CW00832567

Pursue
Happiness
And Get
Enlightened

RAMESH S. BALSEKAR

Books by Ramesh S. Balsekar

- Pointers From Ramana Maharshi (2008)
- Celebrate the Wit & Wisdom - Relax and Enjoy (2008)
- Does The Human Being Have Free Will? (2007)
- Enlightened Living (2007)
- A Buddha's Babble (2006)
- A Personal Religion of Your Own (2006)
- The Essence of The Ashtavakra Gita (2006)
- The Relationship Between 'I' And 'Me' (2006)
- A Homage To The Unique Teaching of Ramesh S. Balsekar (2006)
- Seeking Enlightenment – Why ? (2005)
- Nuggets of Wisdom (2005)
- The End of The Seeking (2005)
- Spiritual Search Step By Step (2004)
- Confusion No More (2003)
- Guru Pournima (2003)
- Upadesa Saram (2001)
- Advaita, the Buddha and the Unbroken Whole (2000)
- It So Happened That... (2000)
- Sin and Guilt: Monstrosity of Mind (2000)
- Meaningful Trivialities from the Source (2000)
- The Infamous Ego (1999)
- Who Cares?! (1999)
- The Essence of the Bhagavad Gita (1999)
- Your Head in the Tiger's Mouth (1997)
- Consciousness Writes (1996)
- Consciousness Strikes (1996)
- The Bhagavad Gita – A Selection (1995)
- Ripples (1994)
- Consciousness Speaks (1994)

Pursue
Happiness
And Get
Enlightened

ॐ

RAMESH S. BALSEKAR

EDITED BY
YOGESH SHARMA

Copyright © 2008 By Ramesh S. Balsekar

First Edition July 2008

PUBLISHED BY

ZEN PUBLICATIONS
59, Juhu Supreme Shopping Centre,
Gulmohar Cross Road No. 9, JVPD Scheme,
Juhu, Mumbai 400 049. India.

Tel: (+91 22) 32408074
eMail: info@zenpublications.com
Website: www.zenpublications.com

Hardcover
ISBN 10   81-88071-46-3
ISBN 13   978-81-88071-46-3

Softcover
ISBN 10   81-88071-47-1
ISBN 13   978-81-88071-47-0

CREDITS
Cover & Book Design by Red Sky Designs
Photographs of the Author by Dheeraj Chawda (p 14, 52) and Colin Mallard (p 20, 86)

PRINTED BY

Magna Graphics (India) Limited, Mumbai
101 C&D, Government Industrial Estate,
Charkop, Kandivli (W), Mumbai 400 067. India.
Tel. (+91 22) 28683738 / 28686658 Fax. (+9122) 28682905
eMail. magna@vsnl.com
Website. www.magnagraphicsindia.com

ACKNOWLEDGEMENT

The Publishers would like to thank Suresh Makhija for providing the recordings of the satsangs; Canta Dadlaney, Jyoti Gyanchandani and Nehal Shah for their invaluable help in transcribing the talks at extremely short notice; Chaitan Balsekar for valuable suggestions and advice; and Dheeraj Chawda and Colin Mallard for providing the photographs of the author.

All rights reserved. No part of this book may be reproduced or transmitted in any form or by any means, electronic or mechanical, including photocopying, recording, or by any information storage and retrieval system without written permission from the author or his agents, except for the inclusion of brief quotations in a review.

CONTENTS

☙

NOTE FROM THE EDITOR   10

CURTAIN RAISER   12

INTRODUCTION   15

ONE
'NOBODY COULD TELL ME WHAT ENLIGHTENMENT IS'   21

TWO
'I PURSUED ENLIGHTENMENT AND ENDED UP
IN FRUSTRATION'   53

THREE
'I PURSUED HAPPINESS AS A SELFISH AIM AND FOUND
MYSELF ENLIGHTENED'   87

FOUR
'HAPPINESS *IS* ENLIGHTENMENT!'   113

'Enlightenment has never ever been a certified event.'

RAMESH BALSEKAR

৯৯

*'What do you think enlightenment
will give you in this life, for the rest of your life,
that you didn't have before?'*

RAMESH BALSEKAR

৯৯

Note From The Editor

۶۵

Happiness and Enlightenment must probably be the two most misunderstood words in the spiritual lexicon. Happiness is routinely mistaken for pleasure in the moment and Enlightenment for a state of permanent bliss, insulated from all pleasure and pain.

Then again, pursuit of happiness is mistaken for pursuit of pleasure, and that *happening* called Enlightenment is actually considered worthy of *pursuit*.

There are those, and there are a great many of them, who believe that the distance to enlightenment is inversely proportional to the pain you inflict upon yourself. These are the ones who "indulge" in austerities.

And there are those who are convinced that if they can snuff out desire, the reward would be enlightenment; not realising that that itself is a desire. Moreover, the arising of a thought – desire – is a biological reaction over which the ego has no control. The problem is not the arising of desire, but the *pursuit* of desire.

And then there are those who think that the path to Enlightenment is through the annihilation of the ego; and that ego spends an entire lifetime trying to snuff itself out. Who is it that is supposed to have an ego? The whole point is to understand what precisely is the ego who wants enlightenment as a means to happiness.

All this would be vaguely comic if it were not so tragic.

What *Pursue Happiness And Get Enlightened* does is turn the whole subject of enlightenment or Self-realization on its head by demonstrating that pursuing enlightenment leads to frustration whereas pursuing "happiness" makes enlightenment happen.

Rames*ji*, using a patient, step-by-step approach, *based on his own personal experience*, simplifies the quest for true happiness. He walks you through the evidence till you can conclude for yourself that happiness is your very nature and a sincere pursuit of that true happiness actually leads you to a state of *sukha-shanti*, happiness through peace of mind – which is precisely what you expected enlightenment to give you! As simple as that. No need for austerities, no need to insulate yourself from day to day life, no jostling with the ego, no giving up and no doing.

In fact, while reading Rames*ji*'s conversations with spiritual seekers published here, it suddenly hits you that the key lies in understanding that the real problem is the sense of personal doership.

Unless you are crystallised into set concepts, you will find this book as refreshing as it is fascinating. For once, your intellect will back your intuition in saying: "Yes, I know this is true."

Yogesh Sharma
Mumbai, July 2008

☙

CURTAIN RAISER

Extracts from the author's recent book *Pointers from Ramana Maharshi*

ॐ

Happiness

"The desire for happiness (*Sukha-prema*) is a proof of the ever-existing happiness of the SELF; otherwise desire would not arise. If headaches were natural to human beings, no one would try to get rid of it. Man desires that which is natural to him. Happiness is natural to him. Man's attempt can only be to get rid of that which prevents happiness from happening.

Dukha nasham = Sukha prapti"

– Ramana Maharshi

[The human being pursuing pleasure, at some point of time, depending on his destiny, comes to the conclusion that pleasure depends upon a desired object, and therefore that the happiness he is seeking cannot be found in the pleasures of life, but in his attitude to life, and, finally, that the happiness he desires can happen only when he has surrendered his sense of doership and purified the ego. Such happiness lies beyond the waking, dream and sleep states. This is the Reality and consists of the original happiness – *nijananda*].

QUESTION How can I do my duties without attachment? There are my wife and children for whom affection and work is necessary. Am I right?

RAMANA Yoga Vasishta says: "Detachment within and attachment in Appearance."

ꙮ

Intellect

"There is a difference between the intellect of man and that of other animals because man not only sees the world as it is, and acts accordingly, but also seeks fulfillment of desires. In his attempt to fulfill his desires, he extends his vision far and wide. The desire for permanency of happiness and of peace bespeaks such permanency in his own nature; i.e. the SELF. That found, all is found. That is realization, the finality, the goal."

ꙮ

"When the real effortless, permanent, happy nature is realized, it will be found to be perfectly consistent with the ordinary activities of daily living."

ꙮ

"It says in the Upanishads that the *jnani* looks forward eagerly to the time when he can throw off the body, just as the labourer carrying a heavy load looks forward to reaching his destination and laying it down."

– Ramana Maharshi

ꙮ

INTRODUCTION

ℰᴗ

When visitors come to see me, the first thing I tell them is that whatever I say is a "concept" – not the truth. I add that anything any sage has ever said at any time in history is a concept, that whatever any scripture of any religion has ever said is a concept. A "concept" is something that is liable to interpretation and therefore acceptable to some people and not acceptable to others. The "truth" is that which no one can deny.

Most visitors, when asked if they think there is something they know which is the truth and not a concept, have no reply. My answer then is that there indeed is ONE truth that no one can deny. An atheist may come to me and assert that he has studied the subject deeply for twenty years, and has a doctorate in 'Comparative Religions', and he is totally convinced that 'God' does not exist. I would tell him that he is entitled to his view because 'God' is a concept. I would then ask him: God may or may not exist, but can you deny that you yourself do exist? This impersonal awareness of BEING, of existing, which no one can deny, is the only TRUTH. It is not capable of any interpretation. In other words, 'I AM' is the only truth. "I am Tom, Dick or Harry" is not the truth. The truth 'I AM' is covered or hidden by the personal ego of the individual.

It is this individual ego who is the spiritual seeker. And the 'ego' really does not exist. When someone tells me that he has come to me in order to have his ego destroyed so that he can be 'Self-realized' or 'enlightened', I would ask him to produce his ego and I would smash him out of existence before his very eyes!

What then is the 'ego'? When I ask this question: what do you understand by the word 'ego', the answer from most people is that the ego is the "identification with a body as an entity separate from the other people, and that this separation is what makes people unhappy." But mere identification with a name and form (*naama, roopa*) cannot really constitute the ego because even a sage who is supposed to have had his ego destroyed also responds to his name being called, exactly like the ordinary person. In other words, the ordinary person considers himself as an entity with a body and name, separate from others, exactly as the sage does! Then what is it that distinguishes the sage from the ordinary person? What is it that makes a sage a sage? The answer is that the sage has the total understanding without the slightest doubt that, in the words of the Buddha, "Events happen, deeds are done, but there is no individual doer thereof." In other words, the ordinary person considers that he or she is the doer of his or her actions and is responsible for those actions: and that, similarly, every person is responsible for his or her actions. On the other hand, the sage has the total, absolute conviction that neither he nor anyone else is the doer of any action, that all action is the divine happening through some body-mind organism and not anything "done" by anyone.

At this stage, the question arises: If no one is the "doer" of any action, who lives his life in this world? Who is it that experiences happiness or unhappiness? Who is it that seeks 'Self-realization' or 'enlightenment' or whatever? The straight answer is that we think we live our lives, but in reality, life is being lived through the billions of body-mind organisms. It is the ego who thinks he is the doer, and experiences happiness or unhappiness. So, in this matter, the basic concept is that ever since a baby is born and seeks its mother's breast intuitively, life has been nothing but seeking, and it is the ego who thinks he is the seeker, the doer, responsible for his actions.

The basis of this concept is that the human being is really nothing more than a uniquely programmed instrument or computer through which the Source or Primal Energy or Consciousness or God (or whatever label you give to the Source – the ONE without a second) functions and brings about actions. In other words, the Source uses the billions of uniquely programmed human computers exactly as you use your computer. You put in an input in your programmed computer and the computer has no choice but to produce the output for which it has been programmed. You could, of course, say that the computer has the "right" to produce the output just as you think it is your "right" to produce your action!

So, what is the programming in "your" body-mind organism, and how does the Source (or God) use the human computer? You had no choice about your parents and therefore about the genes or the unique DNA in your body-mind organism; nor did you have any choice about the environment in which you were born and in which your body-mind organism has been receiving its conditioning from day one. The unique DNA and the environmental conditioning together form the "programming" in your body-mind computer.

It may seem shocking that the human being, who is supposed to have been created "in the image of God", is being reduced to a programmed computer. But let us not forget that the human being is basically an object – a species of object that, together with thousands of other species of objects, form the totality of manifestation. And what functions through the billions of human computers is the Source or God or primal energy, producing through each human computer exactly that output or action that is supposed to happen according to the Will of God (or Source) or according to, let us say, Natural Law or Cosmic Law. This is not unlike the fact that electricity, an aspect of the primal energy, functioning through each electrical gadget produces that which the particular gadget has been designed to produce.

How does the Source (or God) use the human computer? According to my concept, the input is a thought that comes from Consciousness, the Source; the brain responds to this input and out comes the output in the form of a reaction in the human body-mind organism. Research has proved that the thought input occurs half-a-second before the ego's reaction. It is therefore obvious that the individual ego has no control over the input, and, of course, the ego has had no control over the programming in the body-mind organism. In other words, the ego has no control over the input and has certainly had no control over the programming that dictates the reaction, which is obviously a biological or mechanical reaction. And yet the ego calls this reaction its own action! Thought is one input; the other inputs are based on the objects to which the senses respond – what is seen or heard or tasted or smelt or touched – over which also the ego has no control. In other words, what happens is that the brain reacts to an input in the body-mind organism strictly according to the programming over neither of which did the ego have any control. And yet the ego says that this mechanical reaction is his action!

An important point is that the biological or mechanical reaction in the body-mind computer is exactly the same whether it is that of an ordinary person or of a sage. If the input is the same and the programming is similar, then the output is most likely to be the same. If the two persons see the same thing or hear the same thing, the output would be the same, e.g. anger or amusement or fear or pity or whatever. There is a great misconception that the Self-realization or enlightenment brings about such a tremendous transformation that the sage becomes a perfect human being: no anger, no regrets and no fear. Then the question arises: if the reaction in the programmed computer of the body-mind organism is more or less the same, what is the difference between a sage and an ordinary man? The answer lies in what happens after the initial reaction happens.

In the case of the ordinary person when a negative reaction happens – anger arises – the ego takes over the situation. The ego says "I am angry; I should not be angry, I am told by the doctor that if I do not control my anger, I shall have high blood pressure and that could lead to a heart attack or a stroke." This is the involvement of the ego in horizontal time whereas the reaction in the body-mind computer is only in the present moment. In the case of a sage, anger arises and may take the form of shouting against the person who caused it. But there the reaction ends and the sage is open to whatever might happen in the next moment. I remember a particular incident when I was visiting my Guru, Nisargadatta Maharaj. Someone asked a question, and anger arose. Maharaj shouted at him, "You have been coming here for six years and you ask a stupid question like that?" The visitor concerned knew Maharaj well enough and he gave a witty answer; everyone laughed and Maharaj's laughter was the loudest: one moment anger, the next moment "amusement"! In the case of the ordinary person, there would have been the identification of the ego with that anger as "I am angry and that man made me angry; therefore, I shall not laugh at that man's wit." In other words, in the case of the ordinary man, the involvement of the ego would have taken place horizontally in time and he would not have been open to what happened in the next moment. The sage lives from moment to moment, the body-mind organism responding to whatever happens from moment to moment, whereas the ego of the ordinary man reacts to the natural, biological reaction of the body-mind organism, and gets involved in horizontal time and is not open to what happens from moment to moment. The ego of the ordinary man is therefore sometimes happy and most times unhappy because of the involvement in horizontal time.

ONE

'Nobody could tell me what Enlightenment is'

৯৯

RAMESH Is this your first time here?

LADY VISITOR Yes.

RAMESH And your name is?

LADY VISITOR Visha.

RAMESH Okay, Visha, go ahead.

VISHA Yesterday when I listened to you, it all seemed so easy. And before, I needed so much striving that I needed to do this, to do that and whoossh...(*gesticulates*).

RAMESH Yes. Look, people who tell you it is so easy – who will go to them? (*laughter*). That is one aspect. The other aspect is they themselves don't know how easy it is. It may be so difficult for themselves and which is more often the case. On the other hand, I am not saying that no effort is necessary.

VISHA Oh yes!

RAMESH Where effort is concerned, two things have to be borne in mind. One, the effort that I am making is truly not my effort. It happens. And more important, I make this effort because it is my destiny to make this effort according to God's Will / Cosmic Law. But the most important thing is not to expect any result from my effort. These are the two most important points and if these two important points are kept in mind... Now I am not talking about spirituality, I am talking about daily living. Whenever we are making an effort, we must keep these two points in mind. Let the effort first happen and of course, when you are doing something, you obviously concentrate on what you are doing. That is the basis. Any effort that is being made, even when a child makes an effort, he makes the effort in order to get something, do something.

To concentrate on what you are doing, trying to do a good job – no problem. But, if you keep in mind that this is a job that is really, truly happening through you and not *you* doing it, then immediately no stress remains in that effort. So where effort is concerned, whenever there is less physical strain and mental stress, it makes the effort so much more easy and at the same time more efficient. The effort without physical strain and mental stress makes the effort that much easier and more efficient for that very reason.

Less physical strain and less mental stress – you will find your work getting automatically more efficient. And more efficient work means better chances of your work succeeding. Whereas "I am doing the work, I've got to do it well" and expecting a good result is exactly the opposite of that. Your work is less efficient and there are less chances of your succeeding.

So what I am saying applies to daily living and also it does not exclude the spiritual thing. That also is the same thing.

So what brought you here, Visha?

VISHA I came here, to India, in December and I have been travelling all around and...

RAMESH You came to India as a tourist?

VISHA Yes, as a tourist. I have wanted to come for a long time. So here I am.

RAMESH What part of the world are you from?

VISHA New York city. That's where I live now.

RAMESH I see, and have you voted for Obama? (*Loud laughter.*) And how long have you been interested in what I talk about? My point is that you came to visit India as a tourist or as a spiritual tourist, visiting ashrams?

VISHA As a spiritual tourist.

RAMESH So basically ashrams.

VISHA Yes, and holy places...Varanasi, Pushkar.

RAMESH I see, I see.

VISHA So I have been on the journey...

RAMESH So, visiting holy places...what do you think it will do for you? And are you visiting only Hindu holy places or all holy places? (*Laughs.*)

VISHA Muslim, Hindu, all of them, yes.

RAMESH You have been visiting all of them. I see. So visiting those holy places – what do you expect to get out of it?

VISHA I thought that I was going to get something but there is really nothing to get from visiting holy places.

RAMESH Are you sure? (*Visha laughs.*) I have not really visisted many holy places but those that I have, I did feel a certain energy.

VISHA Yes, you do feel a certain energy.

RAMESH So I feel that there is nothing wrong with people visiting holy places with the idea of sharing that energy. But that's it. That is all. Not as someone keeping a record of 'all the places I have visited', ticking them off. (*Laughter.*) That's not the idea at all. So is your experience that you find a special sort of energy in these places?

VISHA Many of them, yes.

RAMESH But apart from that, did you expect to get anything out of them? And be honest.

VISHA And be honest! I am going to say yes, yes. You come to India on a spiritual quest, thinking that you are going to get something.

RAMESH Yes. So what is that something that you expect to get?

VISHA Well, supposedly that something is enlightenment.

RAMESH What do you think enlightenment will give you in this life, for the rest of your life, that you didn't have before? That is my focal question. That focal question is based on several factors.

What am I going to get for the rest of my life, in this life...which means I am not concerned with the past life and I am not concerned with the future life. This is the only life I am concerned with. This is the only life Ramesh is concerned with. This is the only life Louise is concerned with. This is the only life Visha is concerned with. And which is one of the points that is really, truly not accepted by most people. So, one, is this and two, *who* is looking for whatever.

There is no getting away from it. So who is the seeker, whatever is being sought. Who is the seeker? Ramesh, Visha, Louise are the seekers in this life – three egos, egos being separate entitites with personal doership. So my point is, what is this separate entity looking for in this life – with the understanding that we are reasonably comfortable in life, for which we have to be grateful to God, and also the common sense to know that the very basis of life is uncertainty? Most of the sayings you hear are rubbish. 'As you sow, so you reap' is bloody rubbish. It's common sense.

Common sense is the only thing you can rely on and it tells you that in any given situation, you are free to do whatever you want. No questions! That is the only sure thing in life. *Once you have done whatever you wanted to do in any situation, what happens thereafter has never, ever been in anyone's control.*

Even if God took a human life, the same rules of life will apply. He is free to do whatever he wants but the results of it will never be in his control. Two, everybody's experience is that having done, whatever he or she had wanted to do in a given situation, the results have always been beyond one's control. But, everybody's experience has been that sometimes I have got what I wanted, sometimes I've not got what I wanted, sometimes what I got was beyond expectation, many times for the worse, sometimes for the better. Isn't that right or is your experience the other way round?

VISHA No.

Louise Sometimes yes and sometimes no.

Ramesh In my experience, what happened was for the better! Do you know I am a very special person in this world? Something that has happened beyond expectation has happened to me which has not happened to anyone else in this world. Isn't that amazing? I'll tell you what happened.

I did my B.A. here, with Economics and Politics. I had nothing to do with Commerce or Accountancy. Then I went to London for a B.Com degree, Bachelor of Commerce, at the London School of Economics. Many people did that. So there, the usual rule was that a graduate who had not done Accountancy was allowed to appear for the B.Com course. But, during that year they had to pass in an exam in Accountancy, because that was a subject that the Arts students didn't know.

So everybody had to appear for an entrance examination. People from all over the world came and it was a very simple exam. The main purpose was to test his control over the English language and the minimum of common sense. So it was an easy exam and it offerd a wide choice because there was no particular curriculum. So we had only two or three questions to be answered from among eight or ten options. And the usual thing was that someone who had done a B.A. from Bombay got partial exemption. This meant that I would be allowed to appear for the B.Com but during the year I would have to pass an exam in Accountancy. And one's eligibility for continuing was subject to that. If I fail in that, then I can't continue. So they always had that partial exemption.

So I appeared for this exam. I wrote a very good paper and I was very happy with what I had done. No questions about that. Then, when the results were declared, someone told me, "The results are going to be declared tomorrow but if you want to know your result today, you would have to go to Professor Plant and he will tell you." So I went to him. He asked me, "Name?" I said, "Balsekar." He looked the list up and alphabetically it was right on top and he said, "Full exemption."

So I said, "Sir, I didn't do commerce in India. I had done my B.A." He checked across the paper again and said "Full exemption." I had no courage to ask him a third time. So when I came out, I told my friends that I've been given full exemption and they said "Are you crazy? No one has ever got full exemption. No one can!" So I told them that I had asked the Professor twice and anyway we would know tomorrow.

So on the notice board the results were declared: 'R.S. Balsekar – Full exemption'. How it happened? God knows!

But the fact remains that I am the only person in the world who has got a Bachelor of Commerce Degree without ever having appeared in any Accountancy examination! (*Laughter.*)

So to get back to the point. What is someone like us seeking in this life, being reasonably comfortable in life, for which we are grateful to God, compared to the millions of people who are living below the poverty line, while we also have the common sense to know that the very basis of life is uncertainty?

The only certain thing is that I have the total free will to do whatever I want in any situation. That is the only certainty. After that, life is uncertainty. Nobody knows what the next moment is going to bring and my concept is that nobody can know the total amount of pain and pleasure one is supposed to experience in this life and that is already pre-determined.

That has been my own belief ever since I can remember. But as I keep saying, for me that is a concept, but for many leading physicians and mathematicians, that is not a concept but a fact based on their calculations.

So, in other words, life means uncertainty. So, living my life with uncertainty as the very basis of it, what does Ramesh or Louise or Visha want in their lives as the most important thing? The answer is obvious – Happiness.

VISHA Hmmm.

RAMESH And there again my concept states, why do we so promptly say 'Happiness'? Because Happiness is the very basis of our nature. Our true nature is happiness, peace. That is why we want happiness. How do we know that? How do I decide that my nature is happiness and peace?

What is the answer, Louise? Because that is what every human being experiences, every once in twenty four hours during his sleep. So my point is, our very nature is seen in deep sleep and in deep sleep the mind is not there, the world is not there. What exists is peace. Happiness, but through peace of mind.

Therefore, what we are looking out for is peace of mind. Peace of mind which we have in deep sleep – I want it during my daily living, not only for the three or four hours when I am in deep sleep. I want it in my daily life. See what I mean? And that is a fact whether you call it spiritual seeking or ordinary seeking.

Even a spiritual seeker – what does he want? His real nature. Spiritual seeker wants his real nature and his real nature means happiness through peace of mind.

I can tell you that from personal experience. These ashrams which you have visited – I doubt if they could dare to tell you this.

But I didn't know that. What you are lucky to know now, I didn't know when I was a spiritual speaker. So for forty years, I pursued enlightenment without knowing what enlightenment was, without knowing what enlightenment would do for me for the rest of my life – but as a matter of course, one sheep following another sheep, one spiritual seeker following another. Some relative of mine was going to a particular guru. He took me along with him.

So I say, for forty years, I pursued enlightenment and what did I get? Frustration. Why did I get frustration? Because I was not clear about what I expected enlightenment to get for me for the rest of my life!

That is why I tell you that it is so important for you to know, whether you consider yourself a spiritual seeker or not, to know precisely what you expect to get.

And there are reasons why the ashrams and the gurus will not tell you. Because they don't know. And they will admit they don't know. Why will they admit they don't know? Because "I don't know what previous life I have had and I don't know what is the next life I am going to have." So they say this is not one life, which is their basic belief. And I refuse to accept that.

Therefore, in the beginning, what am I concerned with? What Ramesh is concerned with is *this* life! See what I mean? So I pursued enlightenment for forty years and ended up in frustration. So after I retired from work, I started my own personal seeking. And then I decided that what I want is happiness for Ramesh in this life.

I am not concerned with making everybody happy or making everybody reasonably comfortable in life. I am concerned only with this Ramesh. And it is selfish, of course. It is selfish, I confess. What I am looking for is totally selfish – happiness for myself.

So I pursued enlightenment for forty years and ended up in frustration. Thereafter, I decided that what I shall pursue is happiness for Ramesh. Totally selfish – happiness for Ramesh – and I ended up being enlightened!

Isn't that a joke? I repeat, I pursued enlightenment for forty years and ended up in frustration. After that, I started pursuing the selfish aim of happiness for myself and I ended up being enlightened.

For one reason only and that is, I found that the happiness which I was looking for was precisely what enlightenment was supposed to give me! But nobody told me that in the forty years! That is why I am telling you that now. Point number two is, whatever I am telling you is my concept, my experience and I am telling you precisely that but the happiness that I am looking for is my concept. What is happiness? – my concept. What is enlightenment? – my concept.

Happiness for somebody may be different and enlightenment for somebody may be different. So if someone comes and says "Ramesh, do you think you are enlightened?" I will say, "Yes, according to my concept."

"Do you still suffer pain?" *Yes.* "Are you still an imperfect human being? Do you still make mistakes?" *Yes.* "Have you got any special powers? Can you be in two or three places at the same time? Can you know what I am thinking?" *No.* "Can you know what is going on anywhere in the world?" *No!* (*Laughter.*) "Well, then how can you be enlightened?" (*Laughter.*)

And that, believe me, is the general impression about enlightenment for most Indian spiritual seekers. So what I am telling you is that I am enlightened. What is enlightenment for you?

First, my two questions, which nobody could answer.

What is enlightenment? More important, to go from there to, what can enlightenment do for me for the rest of my life? And what do I want? Personal happiness for me, in daily living, that which exists in deep sleep as my nature.

Now I'm clear about what I want. What I am looking for is that happiness through peace of mind which exists in deep sleep and therefore is my true nature – I want that in my daily life, throughout the day. Very clear.

And what is enlightenment? Enlightenement is that which will give me this.

So first I have to find what I am looking for and from that I will know what enlightenment is. See, it is a reverse process. A seeker is supposed to seek enlightment in order to get something but he does not know what.

So the question then is, what is it that I want for that which is happiness through peace of mind throughout the day!

And the next question is, what is the very core of daily living, throughout the day?

What does one mean by daily living? It's not as vast as it may seem. If we go through one's daily living it doesn't seem like a tremendous thing. It is a tiny little thing which can be analysed. What is one's daily living? Routine! Daily living is 95 per cent routine. A routine based on dealing with the other. Daily living is the routine of my relationship with the other. The other may be my parents, my wife or a close relative or a neighbour or someone connected with my business or occupation or a total stranger. In rare cases, even a stranger.

And my happiness depends on my relationship with the other. So my daily living means my relationship with the other and on that depends my happiness. So it is a totally reverse process. So I want happiness through peace of mind, happiness throughtout the day. This means I want happiness through peace of mind with the other, whoever the other is.

That is the focal question I came to. My next question was, what has been the basis of my relationship with the other which has not brought me the happiness?

It is so bloody simple. All you have to do is to see life as it is, in total freedom and honesty. Therefore the question at this moment is "What is the basis of my relation with the other, whoever the other is, which has not brought me the happiness which I am seeking?"

The answer to that is obvious. Anyone who honestly thinks about that must come to the same conclusion. Why? Because that has been the basis of his relationship from the earliest moment in life as brothers and sisters.

So the basis of my relationship with my brothers and sisters has been the same for the rest of my life and that is rivalry. Sibling rivalry is what they call it in the subject of Psychology. Even among little brothers and sisters, there exists rivalry. I can't imagine, except in maybe some rare species, where someone says, "Someone has given me this. I will not eat it. I will give it to my brother. At least half of it."

Can you imagine it? So rare to expect that I would prefer to forget it.

What would most people say? "Aah! I'm so happy my brother is not here! Now I can eat it and I've eaten it. Not only that, but I had the additional pleasure of telling my brother what I had when he was absent."

I'm talking about facts of daily living. Isn't that right? The additional pleasure of seeing my brother cringe. And that has been the basis of every human being. Relationship with the other in daily living has been 99 per cent based on suspicion and rivalry.

LOUISE And that doesn't bring happiness.

RAMESH Suspicion and rivalry for those who are known to me and suspicion and potential enmity towards a stranger. A stranger – is he going to be a friend or a foe?

LOUISE And this attitude doesn't bring any happiness.

RAMESH It *cannot* bring happiness. And that has been so, almost at any place in the world, and at any time.

That was clear. So on that basis, I decided that my search for happiness, which existed in deep sleep, is according to God's Will and is supposed to remain in deep sleep.

God never intended that my happiness in deep sleep be enjoyed by me in daily living. So I came to the conclusion that God never expects any human being to be happy – maybe a rare one, but I am not concerned with that. So God does not expect me to be happy in this life.

I thought a lot about it. I just couldn't get away from it. The only way I can have the original happiness of my true nature, which is only in deep sleep, in daily living is if my relationship with the other is totally harmonious.

What the religions have called and never understood is 'universal brotherhood', in relation to someone close to me or a complete stranger. Universal brotherhood which can never happen.

But when I truly surrendered, the answer came to me from outside and by 'outside' I mean from God. And the answer was short. The answer was "You're wrong. I expect every human being to be happy. To be happy is every human being's birthright. But that one thing on which it depends, the human being is not prepared to accept. And that is the basis of every religion." That is the answer I got. "You're wrong, I do expect every human being to be happy. That happiness depends on one thing which the human being is not prepared to accept! And that is the basis of every religion."

That is the answer I got. So one thing was certain. My search for happiness had started. There is no doubt now that I am supposed to be happy. And in order to be happy, I knew that my relationship with the other had to be totally harmonious. And that, I quickly understood about what God meant. The basis of every religion is universal brotherhood, which means harmonious relationship with the other. But it has not been happening.

What is the one thing which the human being had to do in order to enjoy this happiness which is the basis of every religion? That was the focus of my search. And then it so happened that somehow the four words in the Bible came to my attention. 'Thy Will be done'. Four beautiful words which when I came across them for the first time, made a very deep impression upon me! A tremendous impression.

'Thy Will be done' – which means that nothing can ever happen unless it is God's Will. And then I am told, that Islam says the same thing. In fact, someone fairly recently told me that the literal meaning of the word, Islam, is 'surrender'. And when someone here told me that, I realised that, that throws the whole thing into an answer.

What does the human being, who is born with nothing and leaves with nothing, have to surrender to God? The only thing the human being has which he can surrender to God is his sense of personal doership. In other words, my will against Thy Will. So I came to the conclusion that the reason the human being is unhappy is because he has not accepted the basis of the Christian religion – 'Thy Will be done'. Because when I say 'Thy Will be done', I say 'what about my will'? That means I don't accept Thy Will.

Islam says the same thing. Hindu religion says the same thing in a much more deeper and powerful manner.

The Bible says 'Thy Will be done' and the Hindu religion says, 'Thou art the doer, thou art the experiencer, Thou art the speaker, thou art the listener.' It looks as if Ramesh speaks, Visha listens. Louise speaks, Ramesh listens. But if all three were in deep sleep or sedated into unconsciousness, none of them would be able to speak or listen or do anything.

Therefore who or what does anything? Consciousness!

Without Consciousness, we are unable to do anything. Therefore obviously it is Consciousness which brings about speaking through one instrument and listening through another human instrument. And that is the basis of every religion.

So starting from the answer which I had got, I got my first firm concept. And at that point, it had seemed to me that this concept that I have, is truly the enlightenment that is spoken of. I said that the enlightenment that is spoken of cannot be any other than this concept of mine and what was the concept?

In my own words, "Everything in the world is a happening according to God's Will / Cosmic Law. How each happening affects whom or how is again according to God's Will / Cosmic Law. Through which body-mind instrument the happening happened, which the society called my action or your action or his action or her action is again according to God's Will / Cosmic Law. The human being is incapable of doing anything because he is merely an instrument through which God functions." So, at that point I knew what enlightenment means, according to my concept. And then I knew that enlightenment was total acceptance of my concept. Through which body-mind instrument the happening happened, whether it hurts someone or helps someone is again also according to God's Will / Cosmic Law. The human being is only an instrument and is incapable of doing anything.

For me, the total acceptance of this concept, whatever any scripture may say, for me that is enlightenment and later on I came to know that the great Buddha's idea of enlightenment was precisely the same, absolutely the same. In his own words, I am told, "Events happen, deeds are done, consequences happen but there is no individual doer of any deed." Exactly the same!

Then I pursued it and I realised that this is a concept which no one is likely to accept. No one has accepted this for thousands of years. This concept which I call enlightenment. Why? Because it is a bloody stupid concept to tell someone that you are not the doer when every moment the society punishes him or her for something he or she did. And for him or her to accept that "I am not the doer"...very difficult to accept. Therefore what did I do? I didn't mention it to anybody. So I did what I did. Pursue my concept and see what happens. Pursue my concept and find out whether what I get is happiness or frustration. The total acceptance that I'm not the doer, and when that acceptance was total, then I found immediately, at once, that the entire load of pride for my successful, good, charitable actions disappeared. A bigger load of guilt and shame, for my actions which had hurt someone, disappeared. And an even bigger load of hatred of others for what they had done to me – that load had also disappeared.

Therefore no more load of hatred for myself or for anyone else. This meant obviously that I am at peace with myself and at peace with the other, whoever the other is.

Why was I not comfortable with the other? Because, with his sense of doership, he could hurt me anytime. But now, there was the total acceptance that no human being can hurt me unless it is my destiny to be hurt. There was no question of even hating a stranger. So it turned out that it was a fact that if I am made to accept totally that no one is a doer, everyone is an instrument through which life happens according to God's Will / Cosmic Law, no more load of hatred. Which means I am comfortable with myself and I am comfortable with the other.

And I decided that, that is the happiness through peace of mind which is the result of the end of the load of hatred. Hatred for myself and hatred for the other.

And the Buddha comes to the same conclusion. Had to. Buddha's concept of "Events happen, deeds are done, consequences happen, but there is no individual doer of any deed." Two – 'What will enlightenment do?' Again the Buddha gave precisely the same answer – "Enlightenment – he is much more accurate – means the end of suffering." He does not say that enlightenment is *Ananda*, Bliss, not even Peace.

Therefore, he says, those who are looking for enlightenment, don't expect bliss and special powers. You can only expect the end of suffering. And what is the suffering that ends? The load of hatred for myself and the load of hatred for the other – that load disappears. And the end of that suffering can be termed as 'happiness through peace of mind'.

And there is one very gratifying thing and that is, I came on my own thinking on this in English and said that the happines I want is happiness through peace of mind.

And what is peace of mind? Being comfortable with myself, never being uncomfortable with myself, never being uncomfortable with the other. And then I am told that in Sanskrit, the Hindu version of the ultimate happiness, for thousands of years, has been *'Sukha-Shanti'*. *Sukha* is happiness and *Shanti* is peace. Incredible! The same two words – incredible. Thinking in English, I had arrived at these two words which were written about five thousand years ago: *'Sukha-Shanti'*.

Okay?

LOUISE Yes.

RAMESH (*Turning to another visitor*) Yes, Anand?

ANAND See, some time back I went through a depression.

RAMESH When did you go through a depression?

ANAND Three months back.

RAMESH Three months!

ANAND Yes.

RAMESH After all your spiritual seeking!!

ANAND Yes and now I'm out of it. In retrospect, I'm thinking that the definition of depression is not accepting responsibility. In retrospect, I don't think I caused it or if I could turn the clock back, I don't think I could have done anything different.

And now too the fact that I am out of it is not due to anything that I did. It came and it went. So, in a way, it connects to the same concept.

RAMESH Where is the connection?

ANAND That it happened.

RAMESH The connection is very clear. Your earlier conditioning was, a list of things to be done and a list of things not to be done. Isn't that right?

ANAND Yeah.

RAMESH Your earlier conditioning of how to live in order to be enlightened was to follow a programme of a list of things to be done and a list of things not to be done. And you found that this could be done. You often did things which you should not have done. You often failed to do things which you should have done.

My point is that, that is what brought the depression. 'I have failed as a seeker.' That is the depression.

See what I mean? But the whole point is, whatever you did or did not do, you were not doing anything. They were happening. Happening through this body-mind organism precisely for the reason that they were supposed to happen through this particular body-mind organism according to God's Will / Cosmic Law.

Therefore, you thought you were doing things which you were not supposed to do. You thought you were not doing things which you were supposed to do.

In other words, the depression was due to not accepting the fundamental concept that no human being can be the doer of any deed because the human being is fundamentally only a three dimensional object through which God functions according to the Cosmic Law. Therefore no action is anybody's action. The human being cannot be the doer of any action. Why?

ANAND Because of his genes and conditioning...?

RAMESH Why is the human being fundamentally not able to do anything? Two perspectives. First, according to me, because the human being is fundamentally only a three dimensional object which together with the other trillions and trillions of objects constitutes the manifested universe. So a fundamentally three dimensional object cannot be expected to do anything.

The other perspective is "Then who lives his life?" This perspective is the "Source or God or pure energy, impersonal energy or Impersonal

Consciousness." The Source, not an individual entity, the Source or Power functions through every inert body-mind organism and brings about precisely what is supposed to happen through that body-mind organism at that time and place.

It is a happening. Therefore no one is really doing anything. No human being has ever done anything.

ANAND Guruji, this understanding and acceptance – the fact that it was not happening then and it is happening now – is in itself not in my control.

RAMESH This is what I call your destiny. Therefore my fundamental point is that, whatever happens to anyone is precisely what is supposed to happen according to their destiny. When does destiny begin? When do you think, according to your concept, does destiny begin?

ANAND Before we are born.

RAMESH When do you think we are born? According to me when conception occurs! The moment conception has occurred, the destiny has started. Whether that conception is going to be born a baby, or whether it is going to be aborted or miscarried, is the destiny of that conception.

Once the baby is born, the destiny continues for every split second, right upto the time the body-mind organism is alive. As long as the body-mind organism is alive, the Source is functioning through that body-mind organism bringing about whatever is supposed to happen. And at the end of that life, how that body-mind organism is supposed to die – natural death or accident or murder or suicide – has already been destined, pre-determined.

And during that life, everything that is going to happen during every split second – everything has been pre-determined.

And what is pre-determined is the destiny of that Anand. And therefore everything that happens, happens through the destiny of the individual concerned according to God's Will, according to Cosmic Law.

The human being can only witness whatever is happening as a movie which is being shown on the screen of Consciousness. Only characters play and the important point is "Who are the characters who are enjoying themselves in the play?" The Source! The Source is playing all the characters in this living movie. The Source has created so many human objects. The Source is functioning as the pure energy or Consciousness or whatever, functioning through every body-mind organism and creating the movie that we are watching. What happens is that we are so concerned with what happens in the movie that we forget the screen – which is what is permanent. The screen of Consciousness. Okay?

ANAND One more thing.

RAMESH Please.

ANAND There is a linkage between thoughts, feelings and actions but since the thoughts themselves are not in our control, the whole linkage is not in our control. I know when I think in a certain way, I feel in a certain way and I act in a certain way. For example, when I was going through the depression, I knew I was going through negative dysfunctional thoughts, that were creating such feelings and actions.

RAMESH Now wait a minute. What is your understanding about thought, thinking and action?

ANAND One leads to another.

RAMESH Give me an example.

ANAND Okay. Thought leads to feeling and to action.

RAMESH Where does the thought come from?

ANAND That's the point. It's not mine.

RAMESH That is the point! What leads to action? A thought leads to action. And no human being has ever had any control over what the next thought is going to be!

ANAND But Guruji, this whole thing of visualisation and positive thinking etc., then that does not work at all.

RAMESH Why does a murderer commit a murder for which of course society will take its normal course? Because the murderer had a thought expecting him to murder somebody. But the murder could not have happened unless it was the destiny of the murdered person to be murdered.

Therefore what does it mean? It means, a thought happens to the murderer. The murderer tries to do the murder but whether the murder happens or not is the destiny of the persons concerned – the murderer and the victim.

Therefore the thought leads to action. Therefore any thought leads to action. There is no question about that. Then where does the unhappiness in the human being come in?

ANAND Taking ownership of the thought.

RAMESH But that everybody knows.

ANAND Or wishing that it had been some other way or not accepting it.

RAMESH No. My concept is what brings unhappiness is not the thought because the thought is not in your control. The unhappiness which a human being suffers is not the thought.

ANAND Sense of doership?

RAMESH No. It's the thinking. I have so many concepts like that. Most important, in fact one of the most important is 'thought and thinking', even with Ramana Maharshi – "The trouble with the human mind is that it is full of thoughts." I say "It can't be." The human mind is not capable of entertaining more than one thought at one time.

The mind cannot be full of thoughts. I am again talking from experience. So what happens is that what is meant by 'mind is full of thoughts' is not full of thoughts, but full of thinking which the ego does. Happening of that thought – not in my control. But when I get involved in that thought – thought in the moment is vertical – and start thinking in horizontal time, that is the thinking which occupies my mind and creates unhappiness.

ANAND Is that also under my control? That is not!

RAMESH Even that is not in your control only to the extent...everything is Destiny. When will that be controlled? When your conditioning changes, that thinking will also change. What is happening now? Fresh conditioning. You have heard what I said. It is the thinking which causes problems. This fresh conditioning can change your exising condititioning. Amend it or alter it or even transform it.

If what I said now is powerful enough to transform your thinking then, there need not be any more horizontal thinking.

A thought happens, takes its action. Very similar again to my concept of the egoic reaction and biological reaction.

There are so many concepts but each concept, I really think is my own because no one has brought them out. The big, big difference is, between the thought and thinking and the other is the egoic reaction and biological reaction.

What does the unhappiness most depend on? I got angry, I shouldn't get angry. I was afraid, I shoudn't be afraid. I was disgusted with him but he is my friend but I shouldn't have got disgusted.

Now that disgust, I am told, when the eyes see something or the nose smells something or the tongue tastes something or the fingers touch something, there is an immediate reaction, positive or negative.

That reaction, according to my concept, is essentially a biological reaction. Your genes and your up-to-date conditioning. See what I mean? But what the ego does is that it gets identified with a biological reaction and gets involved in it.

What happens? My eyes see something, my ears hear something – anger may arise! I see it as anger arising in a body-mind organism over which I have no control. Also, the arising of that anger is a happening according to my destiny.

Therefore, that arising of anger, takes its course and I have to accept its consequences which is part of the destiny of this body-mind organism.

So, anger may arise, fear may arise, disgust may arise, surprise may arise, compassion may arise. All these are feelings, which are biological reactions depending on your genes over which you have no control and your up-to-date conditioning over which also you have no control.

So, whether anger arises or fear arises or disgust arises or surprise arises or compassion arises, I witness it as a biological reaction in a body-mind organism which happens to be mine and I have to accept the result of that happening. There is no question of getting involved in that, personally getting involved in that, which is what happens in the case of an ordinary person.

How does the ordinary person, the ego, get involved in what is called a biological reaction?

Anger arises and Louisa says "I was angry. I shouldn't get angry! If I get angry, my blood pressure rises, my doctor has told me that I will get a stroke or a heart attack. I must not get angry!" "I was afraid. I shouldn't be afraid." "I want to be great like my friend. But what can I do if my genes are such that I am not a great person? Nothing I can do."

On the other hand, a positive reaction may arise. I see some anger arising in some body-mind organism, fear arising in another, sympathy arising in the third and compassion arising in me depending on whatever the eyes have seen or the ears have heard. The ordinary person says "I was angry", "I was afraid" and gets involved. Compassion arises and the ordinary person says "I am a compassionate person."

Guilt and shame in the negative involvement and pride in the positive involvement. Nonetheless, involvement!

That is the difference between a man of understanding and one who hasn't got the understanding.

To distinguish clearly between an egoic reaction, which is envy and jealousy whereas this is a biological reaction.

Therefore how do I live my life? In any given situation I do whatever I like, whatever I decide to do, knowing that whatever decision I make depends on two factors – my genes and my up-to-date conditioning over neither of which I have had any control. Therefore though it is apparently 'my decision' it is a decision based on two factors – which God infused in this body-mind-organism.

Therefore, whatever I have been doing all my life, whatever I have just done, is precisely what God expected me to do. Whatever I have done is based on two factors which God infused in this body-mind organism.

Therefore, without the slightest doubt, whatever I thought I had been doing was actually God functioning through this body-mind organism and bringing about a happening which the society considered my action, judged it as good or bad, rewarded me or punished me.

Reward from the society was pleasure in the moment and punishment from the society was pain in the moment which I had to accept as my destiny. So, at any given moment, I do whatever I like knowing that it is really not my action but God's action but waiting for the result of that action which may be pleasure or pain according to God's Will and which I accept. I accept whatever the result without any regrets about the past which is dead; no complaints about the present because I have already exercised my total free will; and no expectations in the future because I have no control over that. And that means no frustration and not condemning anybody for anything, neither myself nor the other.

The result can be only one thing – 'Sukha–Shanti'. Happiness through peace of mind.

ANAND Is it accurate to say that a thought is a happening which leads to an action which is all a part of destiny. On the other hand, thinking is something which I do...

RAMESH But also a part of your destiny!

ANAND But that leads to suffering. Suffering which was your destiny. That is why you did the thinking...

LADY VISITOR Ramesh, so for the thinking mind to end the conditioning has to be totally transformed.

RAMESH Whatever you do depends on two factors – your genes and your up-to-date conditioning, to the extent that the reaction is based on the genes, nothing you can do except accept that you are not the doer. But the conditioning to be able to accept that you are not the doer is the fresh conditioning that is happening. This fresh conditioning which is happening has the power to amend or alter or transform it. I have seen that happen.

VISITOR Yes.

RAMESH And the thinking mind keeps reducing and reducing itself. It can be gradual. The thinking mind says 'I am the doer' but when the understanding goes deeper and deeper that you are not the doer then you will find that the involvement becomes less frequent and less intense everytime but the process is a time process until the understanding is total. But the functioning of the understanding may take some time.

In a conceptual scale of zero to ten, as the understanding goes deeper, from zero to ten, your actual experience will be – involvement is bound to happen. The involvement happens and continues till the conceptual stage of seven, eight, nine, ten but at some point, even the intellectual understanding, make no mistake, has the power to arise and cut off the involvement.

Therefore cutting off the involvement is not your responsibilty. Involvement may happen, and it will happen, but your actual experience will be that the involvement happens to be cut off at a certain point.

And when that is your experience then you will find yourself relaxing, merely witnessing the involvement getting cut-off. The involvement becomes less frequent, less intense, which is very encouraging or it can be an obstruction also… "When is it going to…?!" And even that is your destiny.

VISITOR And that is involvement.

ANAND When does Grace come in?

RAMESH Grace comes in when your destiny is supposed to change. Grace cannot change your destiny. When the destiny changes, religion gives it a name – Grace.

GIRI I am doing business. I have a small little shop. Prior to that I was making documentaries on temples.

RAMESH You look like a film-man.

GIRI Oh thank you. I would love to become one and make more money with your blessings. I heard you say that in deep sleep state, according to the general understanding, I wouldn't know if I am dead or alive.

RAMESH That is the point.

GIRI So where does this happiness, *Sukha-Shanti* – where do I comprehend them?

RAMESH You can't. That is why the Source is the lone Reality. There can't be two Sources. So for you to understand the happiness of the Source there have to be two Giri's.

GIRI So there is nothing to know.

RAMESH Exactly. This is a concept and that is why I keep saying that. Therefore the concept is that at the moment I am not as happy as I would like to be. Therefore the whole focal point is, what do I have to do to be happy?

GIRI And you said that on a scale from zero to ten, the involvement is cut–off, which is not in my hands.

RAMESH Again, which is according to Destiny.

GIRI In that sense, am I not doomed in my pursuit of enlightenment or whatsoever we may call it?

RAMESH That you are a seeker, seeker seeking happiness through peace of mind – that leads us to this concept of non-doership. And the process of this doership is what we call freedom from involvement. And the process of this non-doership, even first beginning and then being accepted is in itself your destiny.

GIRI Is there any acceptance?

RAMESH In the case of most people – they are not interested! They think this is wasting their time. Therefore what is the general picture? The general picture, Giri, is that as soon as the newborn baby is born and seeks its mother's breast intuitively, my point is that the human being seeks happiness. For the baby – the baby does not think, therefore the natural happiness and for the baby, happiness means mother's milk. Then the baby grows up into a schoolboy, and what is happiness for the schoolboy? Love from the parents at home, success in the classroom, success in the playing field.

The boy grows up into an adult, and the adult decides – so many pleasures in life! Therefore the adult pursues pleasures in the belief that he is pursuing happiness.

And the destiny of most people is to continue to do that. And die a frustrated death. But it is the destiny of a few people, like us, for whom a thought happens – I know what pleasure is, I am reasonably comfortable in life for which I am grateful to God and still why do I have the deep feeling that I am not happy? And then a seeker is born. Therefore, I confess, that what I am saying is not for the ordinary person or else they will say what about those living below the poverty line?

Therefore the very fact that we are seeking happiness, is a special destiny, as God's favourite. *Allah ke pyare!* We are God's favourites. Why? According to God's Will / Cosmic Law, the basis of which we can never understand. And why can't we understand? Because God's Will / Cosmic Law concerns the entire universe, for all times. Something so vast and complex – the human being cannot understand. We can only accept – Thy Will be done.

So some of us have that feeling that I know what pleasure is and even if I get all the pleasures I still don't have the happiness.

And then the most important conclusion happens – the happiness I am seeking is not to be found in the pleasures of life, nor in the flow of life, but in my attitude to life. My attitude towards life means my attitude towards the other. And therefore what has been my attitude? And there the whole cycle starts.

GIRI But the real happiness is not knowing it?

RAMESH The real happiness is our natural state.

GIRI And that's not knowing, in the case of the newborn baby?

RAMESH Not caring. Not wanting any pleasure – that is the ultimate state.

GIRI Bless us. Thank you

RAMESH Ultimately we realise that – what am I seeking? Happiness. The one who is seeking doesn't really exist. Ramesh is the one who is seeking happiness. Who is Ramesh? Ramesh is the Impersonal Consciousness identified with this particular name and form as a separate entity, with a sense of personal doership, called the ego. So it is the ego who is seeking happiness only so long as the ego is alive. And once the body is dead, the ego in life, in relation to the other, is no longer needed. When the body is dead, the ego is not needed. The identified consciousness is not needed and the identified consciousness again becomes the impersonal consciousness. That is the process which has been going on for millions of years.

GIRI So I play no role?

RAMESH What brought you here?

GIRI I had heard about you and read about you. I have been wanting to come. Though I had come to Bombay a couple of times I didn't know about your whereabouts. I'll call it Destiny. Thank you.
My father was here about ten days back so when I spoke to him about you, he said "Why don't you go and meet him?" He gave me the address and that is how I am here. The pleasure is mine. Thank you.

RAMESH Why bother? Let life flow.

ॐ

Two

'I pursued Enlightenment and ended up in frustration'

ℬ

RAMESH So, your name is…?

DOUGLAS My name is Douglas.

RAMESH Which part of the world are you from?

DOUGLAS All of it! But I was born in California. The last seven years I have been living in Hong Kong.

RAMESH You know, what I talk about is far from Philosophy.

DOUGLAS Cool, that's cool.

RAMESH I talk about happiness in daily living.

DOUGLAS Good, that's what I came for.

RAMESH Are you retired or working in Hong Kong?

DOUGLAS I was working there for the last seven years and I recently sold my company and now I am here to...

RAMESH How long have you been interested in what I talk about?

DOUGLAS May be my whole life.

RAMESH My question to you then is, all your life what have you been seeking?

DOUGLAS Happiness!

RAMESH I entirely agree!

DOUGLAS But the problem with that is this issue of money.

RAMESH Money? Money is a problem...?

DOUGLAS Money is no problem...

Ramesh: Then what are you seeking?

DOUGLAS I am seeking happiness. But in order to live in this world, you need money. You have to work for money.

RAMESH Wait a minute, wait a minute. You know, some two years ago, there was a research done by the professors of the London School of Economics. They made a responsible research into the relationship between money and happiness.

DOUGLAS What did they find?

RAMESH The heading of the article was: "Did you know that the

Bangladeshis are the happiest people in the world?"

DOUGLAS (*Laughs.*) I am not surprised.

RAMESH Do you know where India lands? Number Five. UK was, I think, 46, I am not sure. And America was 135. A responsible body did the research. Therefore, my question is: What is the happiness Douglas is seeking? That is the focal point on which I talk about. Now your first question please...

DOUGLAS It's similar to what we are talking about now. But it seems like, up until this point of my seeking, there's always been this balance that I'm seeking where whatever I do has to have some kind of monetary reward at the end...so how do I find the happiness in doing and also getting some money to exist in this world and be in happiness? I'm a very happy person. But now I'm realizing that I don't want to work because I *have* to work, for money. I want to work because I love to do whatever it is that I want to do. So my question is, does the balance lie in just simply being happy no matter what you are doing...?

RAMESH Wait a minute. My question to you would be, what do you think is the happiness that someone below the poverty line is seeking? My focal question to you Douglas is, what does Douglas or anyone like us, by the grace of God, reasonably comfortable in life, and who also has the common sense to realize from personal experience that the very basis of daily living is uncertainty, what is the happiness he is seeking?

Everything is uncertain. And, along with that, the peculiar thing: the basis of life is uncertainty and yet every human being has had the total free will to do whatever he or she wanted in any given circumstances. These are the two basic facts of life.

Fact number one: every human being has the total free will to do whatever he wanted in a given situation – legal or illegal, moral or immoral. In other words, what I'm saying is, someone like you and me has always had free will; every psychopath, in any part of the world, at any time, has also had the same free will.

Fact number two: no one ever had any control over the result of his action. Part of the basic uncertainty of life. I repeat: Fact number one, I have always had total free will. Fact number two, nobody ever had any control over the result of his action. Both basic facts about which no one can do anything. So whatever we talk, whatever we think, whatever we want, whatever we are trying to get, is based on these two basic facts.

So in these two basic facts, what is the conclusion you come to? The only conclusion you can come to is that the human being does have total free will to do whatever he wants to do but that free will is worthless in practice! Isn't that the conclusion?

And what is everybody's experience? Everybody's daily experience is he does whatever he feels like doing in any given situation and everybody's experience is that one of three things has happened. Everybody's experience from the beginning of time is, he has just done whatever he felt like doing; thereafter no one ever had any control over the result of his action. And what is everybody's experience? And I mean everybody's? Sometimes I have got what I wanted, sometimes I have not got what I wanted – over which no one ever had any control – and sometimes what I got was beyond expectation – many times for the worse, sometimes for the better. See what I mean? No matter which of these three things happen, no human being ever has had any control. In fact, even if God took human birth, as that human being, God too wouldn't have any committed control over the result of his action.

And thereafter what happens? Again, everybody's experience: all that the society has ever been able to do at any time, anywhere, is to consider what had happened as my action. In other words, I have just done whatever I felt like doing; one of three things will happen over which I have no control, and that which happened over which I had no control is what the society will consider as my action, judge it as good or bad, according to existing social regulations and legal provisions, decide whether it is good or bad and reward me or punish me. Reward from the society has meant pleasure in the moment; punishment from the society has meant pain in the moment.

I have just described to you and analyzed for you the daily living of the human being from time immemorial. In other words, the human being is free to do what he wants but no one has any control over whether what he has done will bring pleasure or pain. That is the basic uncertainty of life over which no one has any control. I repeat, every human being has total free will to do anything, but whether what he has done, whatever his intention, whether it will bring him pleasure or pain has never ever been in his control. You never thought along these lines, have you?

DOUGLAS It's not necessary, not something that I can intellectualise, but I can feel it...I understand the truth in it.

RAMESH That is my point. It's enough to feel the truth in it. Nobody has thought about it. But this is a fact of life.

DOUGLAS Yeah, I never looked at it that way.

RAMESH So, this is my focal question. What is the happiness one is seeking – if you are someone like Douglas or Ramesh or David who is reasonably comfortable in life, for which he has to be grateful to God or the Source; and who also knows from practical experience that he has no control over what the next moment will bring, as a result of what he has done or what someone else has done; who knows that no one has any control over the total amount of pleasure one is supposed to experience in one's life, the total amount of pain one is supposed to experience in one's life – and my concept is that that is pre-determined. One of my basic concepts is, how much pain, how much pleasure every human being is supposed to experience in life is already pre-determined.

That is one of my basic concepts. In other words, the movie of life is already in the can and we are watching the movie, frame by frame by frame, whereas the whole movie is already there and you can never know what is going to happen at what time to whom.

In these circumstances, my focal question is, "What does Douglas or anyone like us, want most as 'happiness'?" This is the point. I dare not ask the question to someone below the poverty line. You know why? He'll say, "Ramesh are you crazy? I am not a greedy person. All the happiness I want is to have enough money for my basic needs...mine and my family's...food, clothing and shelter. That is all." So now, I'm talking to someone who has risen from that level to a level where he is reasonably comfortable in life. What is the happiness he wants? What is the happiness that Douglas has been seeking? And you say that you don't know. That is what you want to know.

DOUGLAS I think that movie is going to just unfold naturally. What I think I have come up against was, may be, I didn't want to be working...

RAMESH Wait a minute. Shall I tell you what you have come up against?

DOUGLAS What's that?

RAMESH You have come up against the basic fact of life that you have no control over what the next moment is going to bring, pleasure or pain, and Douglas doesn't like it!

DOUGLAS (*Laughs.*)

RAMESH Tell me, am I right or am I wrong?

DOUGLAS I don't think you are right there. I accept whatever happens, pleasure or pain.

RAMESH Then, what is Douglas complaining about?

DOUGLAS He is not complaining. He is just wondering…

RAMESH Okay, okay. You are not complaining…

DOUGLAS I would just love to pick up a flute and go travel through the world and do whatever I want. But it requires money.

RAMESH Supposing you had money to travel around the world any number of time, then would Douglas be happy? Douglas has enough money, from your own point of view, to travel all over the world any number of times with one girl or two girls or any number of girls…

DOUGLAS It's not like that. It's more about…

Ramesh So he has that money and Douglas thinks that that should make him happy. See what I mean?

DOUGLAS I do.

RAMESH My starting point, Douglas, is something over which you have never thought about. My starting point is that someone like us has to come, from his own experience, to the stage where he has accepted the most important conclusion to come to before facing this question: 'What I want most is Happiness.' Even to be able to face that question, someone like us has to come to that situation where he puts the question to himself. Which is: "I know what pleasure is, I know that there are many pleasures which I have not experienced. Even if I have experienced all the pleasures available to me in the world, I would still be seeking happiness."

DOUGLAS Which is available to you right now…

RAMESH Yes! That's why I make bold to talk you. I make bold to talk to you, not parroting someone else's opinion but from my own personal experience. And what is the experience?

What does Ramesh, by God's grace reasonably comfortable in life, who also knows from his personal experience that even if he has enjoyed all the pleasures in life, he knows what pleasure is – it's only a question of extent or intent, the depth of the pleasure or the extension of the pleasure, it is still pleasure. Ramesh knows what pleasure is, and yet Ramesh is seeking happiness.

The most important conclusion I came to is – and that conclusion is the basis of my further research into personal happiness – "I know what pleasure is and yet I'm seeking happiness."

Therefore, I repeat, the most important conclusion has been that, as far as I am concerned, the happiness I am seeking has nothing to do with pleasure in life. What is more, the happiness I am seeking has nothing to do with life at all. The happiness I'm seeking has nothing to do with the happening of life, with the flow of life, because the flow of life, the happening of life, can only mean pleasure or pain, pleasure or pain – immediately in the moment or the total pain or pleasure I'm supposed to experience. That also I have no idea.

Nobody can have any idea whether the next moment will bring pleasure or pain. No one can know the total amount of pleasure and pain he is supposed to experience in life. The basis of this life is uncertainty. So in these circumstances, what is the happiness I am seeking? The most important conclusion is, the happiness I am seeking is not to be found in the flow of life. The flow of life can only mean pleasure or pain which I know. Therefore the most important conclusion is, the happiness I am seeking depends not on anything happening in the flow of life but in my attitude to what happens in the flow of life. And therefore my happiness depends on my *attitude* towards what happens in the flow of life. Therefore the happiness I am seeking is my own subjective personal experience.

The newborn baby seeks its mother's breast intuitively. What is the newborn baby seeking? Happiness. Happiness for the newborn baby means mother's milk. The baby grows into a school-going young man and for the schoolboy happiness means love from the parents at home. And if someone in the modern day finds his parents always quarrelling, that boy can never be happy. So for the schoolboy, it means happiness at home, success in the classroom, success in the playing field. Then the boy grows into an adult and then the adult says, "Oh life is so wonderful, there are so many pleasures in life!" And so the average adult pursues pleasures with the mistaken notion that he is pursuing happiness.

And very few people like us, by God's grace, God's favourites, I say, face this question: what is the happiness I am seeking? Therefore they stop pursuing pleasures – "No, I don't want pleasures, I am still seeking happiness" – so those few people have to come to the conclusion that, "The happiness I am seeking is to be found not in the flow of life but in my attitude to what happens in life." I repeat, it is the most important thing.

So, unless someone comes to that conclusion from his own experience, he cannot be the seeker of happiness that I am talking to. See what I mean? Therefore if you say, "In other words Ramesh, what you are saying is, your teaching is not meant for me." I entirely agree with you. Man in the street, let God be concerned with him, not me. I am concerned with *my* happiness in *this* life.

DOUGLAS In this moment...

RAMESH Not really. This life, not just in this moment; for the rest of my life. And the biggest uncertainty is that I don't know whether my life means one more day or fifty more years. That's another part of the uncertainty. So, the most important conclusion is, I repeat, "My happiness depends on my attitude to life and not what happens in life."

Then my really big question – I came to almost a dead wall – 'my attitude to life' is vague. What do I really mean when I say 'attitude to life'? I can't take the next step unless I know precisely what I mean by my 'attitude to life'. It took me a long time and lot of thinking, lot of misery to come to the conclusion that my attitude to life can only mean my attitude towards the other. Daily living, morning till night, means nothing but my relationship with the other. Me and the other. Morning till night. The other may be my parent or wife or son or relative or neighbour, someone connected with my business or occupation or a total stranger. So the basis of daily living is relationship with the other. The other may be the closest relative or the farthest stranger. Therefore my happiness depends on my relationship with the other, whoever the other is, closest relative or the farthest stranger. That's the conclusion.

From there the next step was quite easy. What has been my relationship with the other, whoever the other is, so far in life, which has brought me not happiness, but unhappiness? See what I mean? I am still seeking happiness, therefore I have not got happiness. On the contrary, when I think about it, what I have got is not happiness but unhappiness. What drives me to seek happiness? What drives me to seek happiness is my unhappiness in the present moment. What is unhappiness? Suffering. Therefore what really drives me to seek happiness is the fact that now, in this moment, I am suffering. There is suffering, unhappiness.

So what has been my attitude to the other so far in life which has brought me unhappiness, not happiness? Each time, I am going step by step because I am talking from my own personal experience. Step by step. First, I am seeking happiness because I know it has nothing to do with pleasure. Then my happiness depends upon my attitude to life. My attitude to life ultimately means my attitude towards the other. My attitude towards the other so far, what has it been so that I can change it?

What do you think, if you have arrived at that point, what would Douglas say has been his attitude towards the other? Morning till night whoever the other is, the closest relative or the farthest stranger, what do you think is your experience? What has been Douglas' personal experience about his attitude towards the other so far in his life, whoever the other is?

DOUGLAS Well, sometimes the attitude has been good and sometimes it has been bad too, so I guess...

RAMESH So what is the basis of that some time?

DOUGLAS The me. It's me...

RAMESH Wait a minute. In other words what you are saying is: sometimes this, sometimes that. Sometimes this means sometimes happiness, mostly that which means unhappiness and sorrow. Suffering. Isn't that right?

DOUGLAS Yeah.

RAMESH So we can forget about the sometimes when you have been happy. Let's focus on sometimes when you have not been happy. So what has been your attitude towards the other in those times when you were not happy, when it brought suffering? What has been your attitude towards the other so far which has brought you suffering? The answer is...

DOUGLAS The unhappiness is within myself...

RAMESH We are only talking about your being happy or unhappy.

DOUGLAS Right. But the point is, it doesn't matter about them...

RAMESH What is the focal question? I am not concerned about my greed. What has been my attitude towards the other, whoever the other is, which has brought me unhappiness and not happiness so that I can now change that?

DOUGLAS No matter what.

RAMESH No matter what. Whoever the other is. And I came to the conclusion, which is not so difficult to come to, if I were honest to myself and I was, I said my attitude towards the other has always been one of suspicion, fear, rivalry...

DOUGLAS Jealousy, hate...

RAMESH You can make it a long list but the basis is still what I said. Fear and rivalry. Fear that you may do some harm to me, fear that you may take away something from me, and rivalry because you may prevent something I want because you too want it. Fear and rivalry. That's the conclusion I came to. My relationship with the other, whoever the other is, is based on fear and rivalry.

How many reports do we not see almost every day that a father has killed his son, a brother has killed his brother over a dispute over property? And what is more, there is rivalry even among little brothers and sisters. For them, what causes it is not important. In daily living there is rivalry among even little brothers and sisters. In Psychology I think there's a technical word for it – sibling rivalry. Rivalry between brothers and sisters, which is part of daily living. Human nature. So, believe me this is a fact.

Douglas, I came to the conclusion that if there is fear and rivalry even among little brothers and sisters is it not part of the human behaviour? Is it not part of human nature? Therefore I came to the conclusion, Douglas, that it is stupid to seek happiness. God does not want me to be happy. That is why God has created my nature such that amongst all human beings there is rivalry and fear of another. This, in addition to the fact that the basis of life is uncertainty. I cannot know what the next moment will bring – pleasure or pain. I cannot know the total amount of pleasure and pain I am supposed to experience in my life and I cannot live my life without fearing the other and treating the other as a rival.

The only conclusion I came to is, it is stupid to seek happiness. Happiness consists in accepting whatever life has brought me so far and not wanting anything more. Therefore, honestly, I came to the conclusion that God does not want me or any human being to be happy. God wants us to be unhappy.

In other words, daily living is imprisonment. We have been sentenced to life imprisonment. Forced to live our lives. We have been forced into life imprisonment for life. So, in this imprisonment for life, the question still remains: what is the happiness I want? And the only answer, Douglas, is that I am imprisoned for life, so I have to live my life as a prisoner and the only thing I can ask is that I am allowed to live my life as a prisoner, with the least suffering. A prisoner can't ask for happiness. So what can a prisoner in life ask for? As little suffering as possible. And what is the suffering a prisoner has to be afraid of? Rigorous imprisonment.

Therefore the prisoner of life, all he has to say is, I am a prisoner, I can't help it. But please allow me to live my life with as little suffering as possible. So what is the suffering? Rigorous imprisonment. So all that the imprisoned liver of life has to ask is, allow me to live my life without the suffering of the rigorous imprisonment. So what will rigorous imprisonment bring to me? If I complain and whine and grumble to the jailer about how difficult he has made my life, he'll say, "Oh is that right? You think you are suffering?" So the jailer will turn simple imprisonment into rigorous imprisonment. And then you will realise.

Therefore again, the conclusion I came to at that moment was that it is stupid to seek happiness. There is no such thing. Impossible. After having genuinely investigated the matter – and that is important, Douglas. So I decided to give up my chase for pursuit of happiness. Not with a sense of even resignation, or a feeling that life is unfair, not as if holding something against God, but as a genuine fact of life. So my surrender was totally, totally natural. In the greatest of humility. Not with resentment. "This is what life is. Simple imprisonment."

Again, I can be grateful to God that I am in a reasonably comfortable situation whereas millions of people are suffering. So, when I have given it up spontaneously and without resentment, perhaps for that reason, the answer came to me from outside, from 'outside' being from God. "You are wrong. It has never been my intention for the human being to be unhappy. In fact, I have given happiness as the birthright of the human being. But that happiness is based only on one factor, which the human being has discarded. That is why the human being has chosen to be unhappy. "Happiness is the birthright of the human being. In other words, happiness is your very nature. But you have discarded that happiness by not accepting the one factor on which it is based. And this factor, the basis of your happiness is really a cruel joke. And that factor is the basis of every religion. Your happiness is based on one factor and that factor is the basis of every religion and yet the human being has discarded it." That's all.

So my next step was quite clear. What is the basis of every religion? And that factor is the basis of every religion. Earlier, after thinking about it, I had come to the conclusion that if the same factor is the basis of every religion, why are there religious wars? Is it not possible for people to come together and have one basis of religion? And my answer was, "No. Otherwise they would have done it." Otherwise they would not have had religious wars for hundreds of years. Wars not only between different religions but wars between different sects of the same religion. Therefore I concluded, there cannot be one single basis for all religions.

But here comes the answer from God Himself, "There is!" So my next step was quite clear. What is the basis of every religion? And then I happened to come across four words from the Bible which I had come across I don't know how many times, and had yet ignored them. The four words from the Bible were: "Thy Will be done". Extremely simple. It's really funny. Can anyone give you a message simpler than that? Thy Will be done. Nothing can happen unless it is God's Will. Simplest of all. Needs no interpretation. And yet, do you know, it's very funny. A young lady used to come here. She and her partner were deeply interested in this. So she suggested to her parents, who were quite well to do and were on a world tour, why not spend a week with me here. So her parents were here. Good Catholic parents, not one of the modern ones not interested in religion. They were deeply interested. And the first time they heard me, they were in a terrible state. Free will for you? They were angry with their daughter for suggesting that they come here. The mother somehow had a feeling there might be something in it. So they came the second day and the third day.

On the third day the young lady tells me, "Look, my father is terribly against you but he comes with me because he says I will be sad if he doesn't come. But my mother, she says, something is happening to her. So she wants to see you without her husband. So can my mother see you without my father, alone for half an hour or so?"

I said, "Yes, certainly."

So she came here one afternoon and we talked more about it. And in about three or four days, she had totally melted into this, into acceptance of this philosophy. But the father was still unshaken like a rock.

There is a Club here, quite close, and many foreigners go there. And I was told, every day people would meet in the Club and the group would form itself, five or six, trying to convert the father into my philosophy. And he would stand firm.

So when they went back, I will tell you a joke, when they went back the father sent a book to the daughter suggesting that she give it to me.

That book, titled *The Will Of God*, was written by someone high up in the Catholic Church, and right across the its front page it announced, "650000 copies sold!". Which means at least a million people must have read it? A million people must have read it because they probably felt somewhat bothered by the Will of God.

So what did the book say? It said, the will of God appears simple but it is not. It needs to be studied. The author doesn't say it but he means it: "I have studied it. Let me give you the benefit of my study." And what is my study? He says the will of God has three aspects – nothing as simple as 'Thy Will be done' or 'Nothing can happen unless it is God's will'. No, no. It said, that the Will of God has three aspects. First there is the 'Intentional Will of God'. According to the Intentional Will of God, people like Adolf Hitler were not supposed to be born at all! They were born because of the 'Circumstantial Will of God'. Finally, there is the 'Ultimate Will of God'. The Nazis had the whole Europe under their domination. In spite of that the Nazis stumbled and Adolf Hitler shot himself dead. That is when the Ultimate Will of God prevailed.

My immediate question was, "You mean to say God didn't have control over the other two aspects of his Will?!" This kind of a thing!

The point I am making, Douglas, is that million or two million people faced the need of something like this to hang on to. They needed it because they never really believed it. They never believed 'Thy Will be done'.

And I am told that Islam says the same thing: *Insha'allah!* (Thy Will be done). And the Hindu religion says the same thing more powerfully. The Hindu religion says, "Thou art the doer, thou art the experiencer. Thou art the speaker, thou art the listener." You see? Incredible.

The explanation is, it appears as if Ramesh speaks, Douglas listens. Gabriel speaks, Ramesh listens. But if all three were in deep sleep, or sedated into unconsciousness, none of them would be able to speak or listen or do anything. Therefore who does anything? Consciousness does everything. Consciousness functioning through one body brings out the speaking; Consciousness brings out the listening through another body-mind organism. Speaking through this and listening through that. Therefore the one who really functions is Consciousness or God. So it is God functioning through six billion human body-mind instruments and bringing about whatever is supposed to happen according to God's Will, and I add, Cosmic Law. And all the religions agree on this.

So when I came to the conclusion that there *is* a single basis of every religion then my next question was very simple: why should it be that almost all people in the world should not be able to accept a simple concept that 'Thy Will be done'. Nothing can happen unless it is the Will of God. The basis of every religion. Why does the average human being find it almost impossible to accept it? It's a fact. I'm telling you this because I'm telling you my personal experience. Why should it be so difficult for people to accept that nothing can happen unless it is God's Will?

When I thought about it, the answer was quite simple. Because it is the experience of every single person in daily life that daily life happens only because the human being has free will. In a given situation, I do what I want to, I suffer or enjoy because of what I have done. I am responsible for my action, and you, the other, are responsible for your action. That is the basis of daily living. How can I accept that I am not the doer? If I am not the doer then I would be irresponsible. In daily living, how can I live an irresponsible life? Impossible. Therefore I have to live my life responsibly doing whatever I feel like doing. Where does God come into it?

So it is this very birthright of free will in the human being which has prevented him from accepting that his free will is worthless both in theory and practice. Actually, he feels free will is the most important thing in his life. Life won't happen unless it was there...which is a fact.

The mechanism of daily living cannot happen unless every human being has had total free will to do anything he or she wanted at any time, under any circumstances. Therefore the very basis of the mechanism of daily living is the human being's free will. Because of that the human being has not been able to accept the basis of every religion. But the fact remains that this is the basis of my happiness. The basis of my happiness is 'Thy Will be done'. Nothing can happen unless it is God's Will.

So the conclusion I came to was this. I had been seeking enlightenment for 30 to 40 years. And I ended up being frustrated. Nobody would tell me what enlightenment it is that I was seeking. More important, what will enlightenment do for me for the rest of my life that I didn't have before? No one could tell me. And my earlier Guru – I had two Gurus – once when I dared to ask him, he was angry. I asked him these two questions. He looked at me angrily as if I was insulting him and then he looked around – not so many people, otherwise I probably would not have dared ask him – he looked around and everybody was waiting for the answer. Nobody dared to ask these questions, but once the questions were asked they were eager for the answer. What is the enlightenment that I am supposed to seek? Two, why should I seek enlightenment? What will enlightenment do for me? So, everybody was waiting for the answer. He cooled down and he gave me an answer. You know what the answer was? What will enlightenment do for you? "You can only know when you are enlightened!" (*Laughter.*) That's an escape route!

So therefore I say now I know what enlightenment is. At that point, when I came to Thy Will be done, when it entered my heart, that is the basis of my happiness. To be able to accept totally, Thy Will be done, Thou art the doer, thou art the experiencer; thou art the speaker, thou art the listener. Totally. So from that I decided, "Now I can tell you what enlightenment is, according to my concept."

Therefore the firm conclusion I came to was: Enlightenment has never ever been a certified event whereas everybody seeking enlightenment has been given the wrong impression that it is. Nobody has wondered who has certified it. But everybody knows enlightenment has to be there. So my first conclusion was, enlightenment has never ever been a certified event. Enlightenment has always been a personal concept.

Therefore according to my own concept, I am enlightened. According to my own concept of enlightenment, I am enlightened. So what has been my concept? Very clear. I wrote it down:

1. Everything in the world is a happening according to God's Will, and I added 'Cosmic Law'.

2. How each happening affects whom in the world, for better or worse is again not according to anyone else but according to God's Will / Cosmic Law.

3. Through which person, which body-mind a happening happens, which the society calls your action or my action or his action is again according to God's Will / Cosmic Law.

4. The human being is incapable of doing any deed.

That is enlightenment. Isn't that clear?

My next question to myself was: having accepted that totally, what is the happiness that I have got? Having accepted this concept of enlightenment, what is the happiness that I have got? That, from my personal experience, was very clear. The happiness I got was the absence of suffering. I had earlier come to the conclusion, without really realising the depth of it, that happiness is something not concerned with pleasure in life. If my happiness is not concerned with any pleasure in life, it means happiness cannot be anything positive. Anything positive can only be pleasure in life.

Therefore, from my experience, I realised that the happiness that I had got was the end of suffering. And what was the suffering? Because I thought I was the doer of my actions I was carrying a load of guilt and shame for my actions which have hurt others and a bigger load of hatred for others who have hurt me. Now that I have totally accepted the fact that no human being has ever been able to do anything, if a happening has happened through me which has hurt someone, it is because it is his destiny to be hurt and God's Will for him to be hurt. I am only an intermediary, a three-dimensional object, an instrument He needed for something to happen.

So what is the happiness I have got? Happiness has been the end of the suffering. What is the suffering? The load of hatred for myself for my actions and a bigger load of hatred for others for their actions. That load of hatred just collapsed. And the end of hatred for myself and the others is a happening which I translated as peace of mind. And you know the real joke? I came to the conclusion, thinking in English, about happiness for myself, that the ultimate happiness which I have got is 'Happiness through peace of mind'. And you know the big joke? The big joke is, a little while after that I came to know that for 5000 years the classical Sanskrit phrase for this happiness has been literally the same: 'Happiness through peace of mind – *Sukha-Shanti*.' *Sukha* means happiness and *Shanti* means peace of mind. Literally the same. Isn't it astonishing? 5000 years ago, they came to the same conclusion! That if you are able to accept that the only one who can do anything is the Reality, and none of the appearances, and every human being is an appearance in the manifestation. The total acceptance of this means *Sukha-Shanti*.

I repeat, I pursued enlightenment and ended in frustration. I pursued the selfish object of personal happiness for myself in this life and I ended up getting enlightened. But according to my concept, don't forget! Not according to any certified event.

DURGANAND You said that enlightenment is the acceptance that "I am not the doer..."

RAMESH Wait a minute. More important, enlightenment has never ever been a certified event. But everybody talks of enlightenment as if it is a certified event! That's why I make it perfectly clear. When you talk about enlightenment, be sure that there is no such thing as a certified enlightenment. It can only be a personal concept. Therefore if I say I am enlightened, I am enlightened according to my concept. But it may be that you don't accept my concept. And that is what happened. Your question will be, "You say you are enlightened. Do you still suffer pain in the moment?" *Yes.* "Do you still make mistakes for which the society punishes you?" *Yes.* "Do you have any special powers to know whatever goes on anywhere in the world?" *No.* "Do you have any special powers of healing?" *No.* "Then how can you be enlightened?!" Isn't that right? How can you be enlightened? Because according to the certified event you can't be enlightened! Yes, go on, please.

DURGANAND So this is a concept?

RAMESH Yes.

DURGANAND And it varies from person to person.

RAMESH Yes.

DURGANAND So there is nothing like absolute enlightenment.

RAMESH Enlightenment is not a certified event.

DURGANAND So this concept you gave is one concept you have on enlightenment...

RAMESH My only concept. Enlightenment to me means: Everything in the world is a happening according to God's Will / Cosmic Law; through which person, through which body-mind the happening happens which the society calls your action or my action or his action or her action is again according to God's Will / Cosmic Law; how each happening affects whom, for better or worse, is again according to God's Will / Cosmic Law; the human being is incapable of doing any deed. The total acceptance of this means enlightenment.

DURGANAND For this definition of enlightenment to work, there should be some concept of God / Cosmic Law. And I have to attribute to this entity, the human concept of Will which is again my own creation...

RAMESH On that you are entitled to ask me, I say according to God's Will or Cosmic Law. What is my concept of God? Part of your question is that. What is God's Will and what is Cosmic Law based on which the entire world and my happiness depends? According to me, the atheist has the right to come and tell me, "Ramesh, I don't believe in God." What do you think my reaction will be?

DURGANAND Depends on what one means by God. Everybody has a different imagination of God...

RAMESH If an atheist tells me, "I don't believe in God", you know what I will tell him? "I entirely agree with you! I agree with you that God cannot exist as one all-powerful, all-knowing entity as compared to a helpless worthless entity like you and me." That is, when the atheist says that, I agree with him. Therefore for me God is the Source. The Source, the Only Reality, the only Unmanifest Oneness, the only Unmanifest Singularity which was forced to become manifest duality. The Unmanifest Singularity, the basis of the manifestation, gives rise to duality beginning with male and female. And duality of every conceivable kind. Wealth and poverty, saint and psychopath, health and disease, good and evil, duality of every conceivable kind. Therefore in life you cannot expect perfection, you cannot expect truth, you cannot expect happiness in life. So maybe your question then would be...

DURGANAND I want to specifically ask, what you mean by one statement that you made that He is not all-powerful...

Ramesh Entity! No, no. He is all-powerful, yes. But not an entity!

Durganand Entity is not a thing...

Ramesh Entity is not a singular all-powerful singularity. We are helpless entities. God is an all-powerful entity, that is what the concept of God is. We are all helpless entities and God is the one all-powerful entity.

Durganand He is also an entity...

Ramesh That is the concept of God which everybody has. And with that, I agree with the atheist. I don't believe in God. Therefore God, I believe, is the Source and the Source is impersonal consciousness or impersonal energy. Why should God have created manifestation at all? Why should there be a manifestation at all? So that people should be unhappy? The answer is, God did not create the manifestation. God was forced to create the manifestation. God as impersonal energy, God as the Source, Unmanifest Source, potential throbbing energy, potential energy. And the potential energy, by the very nature of potentiality, was forced to activise itself some time; otherwise it would have been dead matter. Therefore potential energy as the Source was forced to activise itself sometime...the Big Bang, fantastic energy, and the entire manifestation. The physicist says that the entire manifestation is a block. Everything is pre-determined. Therefore the Unmanifest Oneness, as potential energy, had to activise itself into manifestation of duality. And when that one Big Bang, the enormous energy, at some time or the other, millions of years later – satyug, this yuga or kalyug or whatever – at the end of that, whatever is left will go back into the potential until another Big Bang happens.

Durganand So, this is also a concept?

Ramesh It is a concept. Make no mistake.

DURGANAND I want to know. This manifestation taking place, this actualisation, from potential to actual, is this real or is it a human concept? Human imagination?

RAMESH It can only be an appearance The only reality is the Unmanifest Reality. Everything else has to be an appearance.

DURGANAND Therefore fictitious.

RAMESH Therefore *not real*. Appearance is an appearance. Is it fictitious? What do I mean by appearance? I mean by appearance, *not a hallucination*. And your fiction could be either hallucination or appearance. Therefore I would not use the word fictitious. I would say it's an appearance. An appearance is an appearance which can be seen; it's not a hallucination.

DURGANAND I am just getting this cleared...it is not a hallucination in the sense it is not purely a construct of the mind. But when you say it is an appearance not a hallucination it is subject to sense perception.

RAMESH Correct.

DURGANAND That's the only difference. But these sense perceptions are again interpreted by the human beings in the mind.

RAMESH In the mind.

DURGANAND Finally it boils down to the interpretation by the mind and the brain.

RAMESH Absolutely.

DURGANAND So, is there a difference between hallucination and appearance?

RAMESH Hallucination doesn't exist. Appearance exists. If you go in the sun and there's a shadow, you would say the shadow is a hallucination? You can see it. You move and the shadow moves.

DURGANAND Let's look at this shadow. I see a shadow of the body and since the eyes have taken that impression of light and lack of light and constructed a concept of shadow. Now the question is, whether this concept of differences in light, is it real or imagination?

RAMESH The only Reality is the Source.

DURGANAND So what I am trying to drive at Rameshji is that both are imaginations.

RAMESH Appearances.

DURGANAND Appearances. Sense appearances and mental hallucinations or illusions, whatever you might call it, they appear to be finally the constructs of the mind and the brain. Therefore it is fictitious. Not real.

RAMESH I would still say that the real has an appearance. The real has a shadow. So the Unmanifest Real has become the appearance which is manifestation. You stand before a mirror and there is an appearance.

DURGANAND Now let me explain my problem. To me both of these things appear to be constructs of my mind. The appearance, the interpretation of sense impressions...

RAMESH What you are saying is, it's a projection of the mind. Agreed.

DURGANAND Now I am worried about an aspect of this, the so-called concept of the Unmanifest Reality. Could it also be a construct of the mind?

RAMESH It is a construct of the mind. Agreed.

DURGANAND The Consciousness, the *atman*...

RAMESH Everything is a construct of the mind.

DURGANAND My problem is...

RAMESH I will tell you. Your problem is, "What the bloody hell is the Truth?!"

DURGANAND Yes.

RAMESH And my answer is, the only bloody Truth in this world is, there never has been a creation. Never has been a creation, never has been a dissolution. When you are in deep sleep, was there ever a creation? When does the creation arise? When you wake up and there is a mind. So whatever creation you see is a creation of the mind. Therefore, for me, Ramana Maharshi is the greatest sage in living history. And Ramana said, "Whatever needs to be said has been said in one verse in Adi Shankara's *Vivekachoodamani*. Verse No. 170." I said, "Wow, what more could he have said?" Whatever needs to be said has been said in Verse 170 in *Vivekachoodamani* by Adi Shankara. And it's interesting. The translation of the original verse 170 in *Vivekachoodamani* is:

> In the dream-state even though there is no contact with the outside world, the mind alone projects the entire dream universe of enjoyer, enjoyment and the object of enjoyment. Similarly, the waking-state is no different. All this world of pluralistic phenomena is but a projection of the mind.

There never really has been a creation. Everything is a projection of the mind.

Durganand There is nothing other than projection of the mind?

Ramesh That is the point. Therefore, just as I agree with the atheist that there is no God, I agree with whatever you say. (*Laughter.*) That it is all a projection of the mind.

Durganand But I want to come to another aspect of this. It's something you were saying long time back. That the only Reality is the impersonal sense of being present. My question was, is that also a construct of the mind?

Ramesh It is. It is. The Consciousness, Impersonal Consciousness...

Durganand Even what Ramana calls I–I, I is also a construct of the mind?

Ramesh Yes, it is. Who is concerned with I–I, I? Who is concerned with the Source? Who wants to know whether there is a Source? Who wants to know what is the Source? The mind! If there was no entity asking this question, an entity with intelligence, who would want to know anything?

Durganand Irrespective of the presence or absence of this entity wanting to know the Truth, does the Truth exist or not?

Ramesh For whom? For whom does it exist or not?

Durganand For itself.

Ramesh If there is no one, for whom can the Truth exist? Who the hell will be interested to know if there is any Truth?

Durganand By itself it cannot exist? By itself, for itself?

Ramesh (*Laughs.*) So who will want to know? Only when you are there...

DURGANAND If I am not there, is it right to say that there is no Reality or Truth?

RAMESH Yes. If you are not there, as it happens at least once in 24 hours, when you are in deep sleep, is there any creation? When you are in deep sleep, every 24 hours, is there any creation? More important, is there anyone to worry about creation being true or not?

DURGANAND But in that state, wouldn't it be wrong to say that a person sleeping does not exist? Consciousness is not existing? Just because there is no sensation, no one to realise, does the absence of that...

RAMESH Who will want to know?

DURGANAND Irrespective of who, I am asking. The question is, irrespective of the object can the subject not exist? Can the subject by itself not exist?

RAMESH Who is going to challenge me, whatever I say? (*Laughter.*)

DURGANAND I am only enquiring Rameshji. There is no question of challenge. I want to really know.

RAMESH Really, the whole point is this: in deep sleep I was not concerned with my happiness. Therefore in my life and living, I am concerned with my happiness in daily living. But when I am dead, when the body-mind organism is dead, what happens to Ramesh or Douglas or whoever? That is important. And my answer is, after the body is dead Ramesh will be precisely in the same state he is every day when he is in deep sleep. Not concerned with anything. Therefore what will happen to Douglas or Ramesh?

First of all, what is Douglas or Ramesh? Or for that matter, what is any individual entity? There are two perspectives. One perspective, he can only be a three dimensional object. So the body-mind organism as a three dimensional object is part of the manifestation. Therefore who can Douglas or Ramesh be? He can only be something connected with the Source. Therefore each human entity, as a separate entity, is nothing but a three dimensional object.

The other perspective is, the Source. Impersonal Consciousness identified with each body-mind organism as a separate entity with a sense of personal doership, is identified consciousness. Therefore every human being as a separate entity with doership as the ego is identified consciousness. When the body is dead, that particular entity is no longer required for daily living to happen, for that entity no more inter-human relationships, the ego is no longer necessary and the identified consciousness again becomes Impersonal Consciousness. Therefore I honestly don't have to worry about what happens to Ramesh. Ramesh again becomes the Source or God.

Therefore I am only concerned about my happiness in this life. What happens when I am dead? Who cares?! The identified consciousness again becomes the Impersonal Consciousness. And the real sensible part, Douglas, is: two rivers join the ocean, two egos have become the Impersonal Consciousness. Two rivers join the ocean. Then no more rivers, only the ocean. And the ocean doesn't care a damn whether one river was the purest Ganga or the most impure horrible thing. Therefore no ego need worry whether it is a good person or a bad person. Because no one can be a good person or a bad person. In both cases it is the Source functioning through one body-mind organism so programmed that only bad things will happen and this has been known as a psychopath. Or the same Source functioning through another body-mind organism known as a sage because it has been so programmed – through genes and conditioning – for only good deeds to happen. No individual doer of any deed. So no one need worry about dying a bad man or a good man.

Durganand You mentioned about the deep sleep state. Is that a state of total ignorance?

Ramesh That is a state in which the question of ignorance or knowledge simply does not arise.

Durganand There's nothing...?

Ramesh The question of knowledge or ignorance simply does not arise.

Durganand Or is it right to say that that is a state of peace? Because the concept of peace also is absent.

Ramesh Peace, for this reason that, that which existed is disturbed when you wake up. So what was it that existed which gets shattered when you wake up? Peace of mind. It's a concept again.

Durganand You said you are not concerned with "What happens after my death. What matters to me is my happiness now." So I am asking if this concept of 'happiness now' is again also a construct of the mind?

Ramesh It is...

Durganand And so there's nothing great about being happy in that imaginary state...

Ramesh Quite right. So don't bother about your happiness.

Durganand So the question again is, these are both constructs of the mind – happiness as well as pleasure. Pleasure at least has a basis on senses whereas happiness which is, you can say, not independent of sense perceptions, is again a mental construct.

RAMESH Absolutely. No question about it.

DURGANAND So why is one superior to the other, preferred to the other?

RAMESH Yes, I would also agree.

DURGANAND Because that seemed to be the basis of your argument this morning...

RAMESH For someone who seeks happiness, the most important conclusion is...

DURGANAND I would say both are equally the constructs of the mind. Whether you are revelling in pleasure or so-called happiness you are living in an imaginary state of mind.

RAMESH So is Durganand not concerned with his happiness in this life?

DURGANAND I am worried about this point. Why should I be concerned about...

RAMESH Don't be concerned! Who prevents you from not being concerned?

DURGANAND All conditioning says that is the thing you are toiling for, that this is the purpose of life. Happiness, to be happy, realised, enlightened...Absence of all these things make you think about it. I would not have bothered about it.

RAMESH The ultimate thing is not to want anything. Not even happiness. That is the ultimate.

DURGANAND But is it not right, this is the definition of happines by most of the people? Not wanting anything.

RAMESH But until you reach that stage you will still be looking for happiness.

DURGANAND Okay.

RAMESH Until you reach that stage. And I would say that possibly even to reach that stage. (*Ramesh hands a small pink coloured booklet to Douglas and asks him to read it aloud.*)

DOUGLAS (*Reading aloud the 'Final Prayer' by Ramesh.*)

> O Lord,
> Give me a state of mind
> So filled with your Being
> That I would not need anything
> From anybody
> Any more
> Not even from you.

RAMESH Not even from you! Not even happiness from you. That is the ultimate stage. That ultimate state is only when the body is dead. And no longer Durganand or Ramesh or Douglas.

DOUGLAS The ocean.

DURGANAND The million dollar question is how to attain that state? Is it possible?

RAMESH Wait a minute. What is that state? That state is when there is no Durganand wanting anything! That state is when Durganand, the one who wants something, is just not there! The identified consciousness as a separate entity, the ego, is just not there.

DURGANAND Is that possible as long as I am living?

RAMESH No, no.

DURGANAND Then it is a meaningless pursuit...

RAMESH Therefore the only meaningful pursuit is happiness in this life. Afterwards, who cares?! That's my whole point.

DURGANAND Even though that happiness is illusory...

RAMESH It is based on your personal concept...therefore that happiness is not anything certified as pleasure. Pleasure is certified. Only this happiness has nothing to do with that pleasure. That is the most important thing.

~

THREE

'I pursued Happiness as a selfish aim and found myself Enlightened'

ॐ

RAMESH So, what is your name?

DANIEL Daniel.

RAMESH What part of the world are you from?

DANIEL Israel.

RAMESH Is this your first visit here?

DANIEL Yes, this is first time.

RAMESH First day, first time.

DANIEL Yes, first day, first time.

RAMESH And how do you know what I talk about? What brought you here? Do you know what I talk about?

DANIEL More or less.

RAMESH Have you read any of my books?

DANIEL Parts. Mainly I know you from friends. A good friend of ours told us to come here. And different people recommended we come here.

RAMESH So, what are you seeking?

DANIEL What am I seeking?

RAMESH How long have you been seeking? What are you seeking?

DANIEL I would say I am seeking happiness.

RAMESH Absolutely correct. You are seeking happiness. Now who is seeking happiness?

DANIEL Part of Daniel who is unhappy.

RAMESH Now, who is seeking happiness? Daniel is seeking happiness. Now, wait a minute. What I talk about is not Philosophy. There are plenty of books on Philosopy. What I am talking about is happiness in daily living...for someone who is reasonably comfortable in life. I am not talking about someone below the poverty line. For a simple reason. If I ask someone living below the poverty line, "What would you want as happiness?" He would tell me, "Are you crazy Ramesh? What I want is enough money for my basic needs – food, clothing and shelter for me and my family." For him that is happiness.

So who is seeking happiness? Someone like Daniel who is reasonably comfortable in life – for which he should be grateful to God and who also knows, from personal experience, that the essence of daily living is total uncertainty.

Nobody can know what the next moment will bring. For example, you may do the nicest thing to help someone or whatever, and yet you may never know whether the nicest thing or the good thing you have done will bring you pain or pleasure. Nobody can know. So my focal point is, "What does someone like us, reasonably comfortable in life, who has accepted, from personal experience, that no one can know what the next moment will bring, pain or pleasure, what does someone like us want as happiness?" No one can know the total amount of pain or pleasure one is going to experience in one's life! Isn't that a fact?

DANIEL So why seek anything?

RAMESH Why seek anything? You are seeking something. Therefore, my focal question is, "What is someone like Daniel, reasonably comfortable in life, for which he is grateful to God, while there are millions of people living under the poverty line, who also knows from personal experience that the basis of living is uncertainty, what is Daniel seeking?" No one can know what the next moment can bring, pleasure or pain and no one can know the total amount of pleasure or pain one has to experience in life which, according to my concept, has already been pre-determined!

In such circumstances, what does Daniel want most as happiness? That is my focal question. You know that from personal experience – you don't know what the next moment will bring, pleasure or pain. Whatever you do, you will never know the result of that. The essence of daily living is that every individual has the total freedom, total free will to do whatever he wants in a given situation.

In a given situation, Daniel has always been free to do whatever he wishes to do, moral or immoral, legal or illegal, the result of which he can never be sure. So in such circumstances what is it that Daniel wants most in life? That is what I talk about! Not philosophy. So from this aspect, what is the happiness you are expecting to get and which you are seeking?

DANIEL You are asking me now?

RAMESH Yes, I am asking you now. I am telling you what is the basis of daily living, which you know from your own life's daily experience. In these circumstances, what precisely is the happiness that Daniel is seeking?

DANIEL It will be hard to know because I don't know what the next moment can bring.

RAMESH And that is what I am talking about. In other words, I don't know whether I am going to get any pleasure in the next moment, and therefore in this moment, whether I am enjoying pleasure or suffering pain, I am still seeking happiness. Therefore, at this present moment, whether I am enjoying pleasure or suffering pain, I am still seeking happiness. So what is the happiness I am seeking, which has nothing to do with whether I am enjoying pleasure in the moment or pain in the moment, over which I have no control? That is precisely what I talk about.

What does someone like us, reasonably comfortable in life, precisely want?

At this moment, what is it that makes you want happiness whether you are suffering pain or enjoying pleasure? What is it that you want? Either way, whether you are suffering pain or enjoying pleasure in the moment. Every human being knows that, that is the fact of life which no one can change. In the game of life, that is the basic rule. If there is pain, I will have to suffer pain. That is something accepted, something that we have to accept. In other words, what I am saying is that the happiness that I am seeking cannot consist of wanting more pleasure and less pain.

What is the happiness I cannot have? The happiness I cannot have is, increasing the pleasure and decreasing the pain that has already been decided by God. Otherwise what is the happiness I want? More pleasure, less pain. You can't have it. It's already pre-determined.

These are the facts of life over which no one has any control. Even if God took human form, he will still have to, in that human form, follow the rules of this basic life.

DANIEL So is the problem in wanting the happiness?

RAMESH No, the problem is in knowing what is the happiness that you want – whether you are enjoying pleasure in the moment or suffering pain in the moment? More accurately, why do I want happiness when I am enjoying pleasure? When I am suffering pain, I know that I want happiness. Even when I am enjoying pleasure, I still want happiness! That is a fact of life! So, when I am enjoying pleasure what is the happiness I want?

DANIEL More pleasure.

RAMESH You cannot have more pleasure.

DANIEL Something that is beyond pleasure and pain.

RAMESH So what is it? That is the point. So I'm going step by step, because I talk to you from my own personal happiness. I sought happiness or self-enlightenment for forty years. And it ended in frustration. Nobody could tell me what is enlightenment. No one could tell me, not even the scriptures could tell me, what enlightenment could do for me, in this life, that I didn't have before.

Therefore, when I retired from work, I decided that I would not pursue enlightenment. It was nothing but frustration. I will pursue happiness. So even when I am enjoying pleasure what is the happiness that I want? So Daniel, from your own experience, what is it?

DANIEL I would say that even when I enjoy pleasure, it is always with a pinch of dissatisfaction because I know it's not going to last.

RAMESH What is the 'pinch of dissatisfaction' when you are trying to enjoy pleasure, Daniel?

DANIEL I would say that I experience it as an inability to completely give myself up to this.

RAMESH You are enjoying pleasure, food or sex or whatever it is. What more happiness do you want from your own experience? What more happiness do you want? And what is your experience Daniel?

It is the experience of every human being that when he is in the midst of enjoying the pleasure, that pleasure gets shattered. You are not allowed to enjoy that pleasure in full intensity. Why? Because something happens and shatters that pleasure. Again, you're suffering in pain. You have accepted that pain. Say, you are a really sick person. You will know from experience that I cannot avoid pain. So if there is pain, you have accepted the pain and you are suffering the pain. What happens is that you have accepted the pain, you are suffering the pain, but something happens and intensifies that pain. You have accepted the pain, physical or psychological. If it is a physical pain, you will take an Aspirin and try to reduce it to the extent possible. Thereafter you have accepted the pain and you are suffering the pain.

What is your experience? Your experience is that something happened and that intensified the pain. See what I mean? And therefore, the happiness that I am seeking is the negative happiness – which is the end of this suffering.

And what is the end of this suffering, this suffering which you would want to be ended, which you call happiness? Shattering of the pleasure you are enjoying or the intensity of your pain being increased. I am talking from personal experience.

I am an intelligent person and I know millions of people are living under the poverty line. God has put me in a reasonably comfortable level in life for which I am forever grateful to Him. I know for a fact that there is nothing I can do to avoid pain or increase pleasure. Therefore I have made up my mind. I have accepted this, that when the pleasure is there, I will enjoy it and when the pain is there, I will suffer it. And yet I am seeking happiness. So what is that happiness I am seeking in spite of accepting totally the pleasure as it happens and the pain as it happens?

When you go into it, this is what happens. I have accepted the basic rule of life. I have accepted that pleasure and pain will alternate. Therefore, because I have accepted the pleasure, I enjoy the pleasure; and because I have accepted the pain, I suffer the pain. But my experience is, over which I have no control, that my pleasure in the moment, gets shattered and my pain in the moment gets intensified.

I have accepted the basis of life but I don't want my pleasure in the moment to be shattered and my pain in the moment being intensified. That is all I want!

And that is the happiness which I am pursuing. See what I mean? Therefore, the most important conclusion I have come to is that the pursuit of happiness does not mean anything positive. Anything positive will only mean pleasure in the moment or pain in the moment. Therefore the most important conclusion is that the happiness which I am seeking is not to be found in the pleasures of life over which I have no control. In other words, my happiness does not depend on the flow of life.

So the acceptance of that is the first step. This leads me to the conclusion that the happiness which I am seeking cannot be something positive. The happiness which I am seeking can only mean the end of suffering which comes in the way of my happiness. My happiness depends on this suffering being ended. And what is the suffering which I want ended? My pleasure in the moment not being shattered and my pain in the moment not being intensified. That is all the happiness I want. Nothing positive. Not ecstasy, bliss etc. Ecstasy, bliss or whatever religion has promised you, can only be in the realm of pleasure because they end. You can't be in bliss all the time and live your daily life. If you're in bliss all the time or if you're in pain all the time – how can you live your life? How can you earn a living?

Therefore, what is the suffering which I want to end? That suffering is my pleasure in the moment being shattered, my pain in the moment being increased. That is the suffering I want ended and that is the happiness I am seeking. The first and most important step in my pursuit of happiness, from my own personal experience, was that the happiness I am seeking is not from the pleasures of life which are momentary, and therefore the happiness I am seeking is not to be found in the flow of life itself! Because the flow of life can only mean pleasure or pain. Most important first conclusion.

Therefore the happiness which I am seeking, the end of the suffering, can depend only on my attitude to life. This is the most important first conclusion.

And that is what was happening – my seeking enlightenment ending in frustration because I expected enlightenment to give me happiness which was in the flow of life. That is why there was frustration.

So this is the base of my pursuit of happiness. I have to find out what has been my attitude to life so far, which has not brought me the happiness but has brought me unhappiness. Step by step. First conclusion: my attitude to life. Second conclusion: what has been my attitude to life so far, which has not brought me happiness but which has brought me unhappiness – so that I can change my attitude to life in order to bring happiness.

So what do I mean by 'my attitude to life'? 'Attitude to life' is a generic term. That is what took me a lot of time, lot of thinking, lot of misery. What was the answer I got? Think for yourself. What does Daniel mean by his 'attitude to life'?

For me it was the most important mental or intellectual exercise. Whatever answers I got, I threw them out having found them very inadequate.

I did this until I came to the one answer which I came to accept as the right answer, the adequate answer. "What I mean by my attitude to life ultimately, in daily living, comes from my attitude towards the other." Attitude to life! People enjoying, people living under the poverty line. My attitude to life is such a vast thing but the important conclusion is, I cannot be concerned with anything that happens because whatever happens is God's Will / Cosmic Law.

My attitude to life can only mean my attitude towards the other, from morning to night. What is the essence of daily living, from morning to night? My relationship with the other! Human relations. Inter-human relations is the basis of daily living. Most important conclusion to come to. The essence of daily living means inter-human relationships, from morning to night. Me and the other! The other may be some close relative, my wife, my parents, my brother or even a neighbour or someone connected to my business or occupation or a total stranger.

Now, what has been my relation with the other, whoever the other is, which has not brought me the happiness but unhappiness?

Look at the crucial thing in this. What do I mean by happiness? You don't know! Now I have come to the conclusion that the happiness which I have been seeking depends on my relation with the other whoever the other is, closest relative or the farthest friend.

So the next question became simple. What has been my relation with the other so far, whoever the other is, closest relative or farthest friend, which has brought me unhappiness and not happiness? That is the crucial question because if I change that attitude, I will have happiness.

So what has Daniel's attitude been towards the other, whoever the other is, closest relative or the farthest friend, which has not brought him happiness but unhappiness? If you are pursuing happiness, this is the question you will come to. So what would you say has been Daniel's attitude so far in life which has not brought him happiness but unhappiness? Your own experience!

DANIEL Oh, so many things!

RAMESH So many things coming down to what? So many things which can be brought down to one centre. So many things, so many different people, is that what you mean?

DANIEL Yes, different relations.

RAMESH Closest relation to the farthest stranger, hundreds of people.

DANIEL Every person reflects a different attitude in myself so...

RAMESH So what has been your attitude towards the other? Hundreds of others during the day or during the year. From your own personal experience. Think all you want and do you know what is the conclusion you will come to, if you are honest with yourself? The only conclusion you will come to, if you are honest with yourself, whoever the other is, closest relative or distant stranger, your attitude towards the other has always been one of suspicion, fear and rivalry.

Suspicion and fear, whoever the other is. If he wants something from you – which you have and he doesn't – he may take it from you. And for taking it from you, he may hurt you or kill you.

DANIEL So it is a kind of an survival instinct.

RAMESH Survival against the other. Fear that the other may not allow you to survive in the circumstances in which you want to survive. Am I right or am I wrong? How many times you may have read in the newspaper about how a father has killed his son or a brother has killed his brother, a friend has killed a friend over a dispute over property, or love or passion or whatever? Isn't that right?

Therefore I say, think all you want, form your own conclusions rather than accepting my conclusion. Better to come to your own conclusion, from your own experience, that your relation with the other is based on suspicion, fear and rivalry.

So if your relation with the other, whoever the other is, is based on suspicion, fear and rivalry, how can you be happy? And this has been the story of inter-human relationships from time immemorial.

What I described to you has been happening for hundreds and thousands of years. A kingdom, two heirs, one heir kills the other in order to rule the kingdom. Whatever the property, fifty thousand dollars or one million dollars, one kills and the other wants to take the whole thing. Isn't that right? Therefore, I repeat, think it out on your own. You don't have to accept my conviction. My conviction has been that the human being is not happy because his relation with the other, whoever the other is, is not harmonious but is based on suspicion, fear and rivalry. And that the human being can be happy only if his relationship with the other is totally harmonious.

And what is totally harmonious? Never being afraid of the other harming me in any way! I don't have to fear the other. That is the totally harmonious relation. And why has it not happened for all these thousands of year? And do you know the conclusion I came to Daniel? The conclusion I came to is that pursuing happiness is stupid because God never intended the human being to be happy. God intended inter-human relationships to be based on suspicion, fear and rivalry. Therefore he made uncertainty as the very basis of daily living. And he made the inter-human relationships to be based on suspicion, fear and rivalry.

Therefore in my pursuit of happiness, the conclusion I came to was that it was stupid to pursue happiness. All I can do is to accept the pleasure and pain as they happen and accept also my pleasure being shattered and my pain being intensified. That also I had to accept and that is the only happiness that I can have.

In other words, I came to the conclusion that God never intended any human being to be totally happy. Isn't that right?

DANIEL I don't know.

RAMESH Where are the loose ends? Why do you say 'I don't know'? Have I not made it absolutely clear?

DANIEL Well, from my experience, this happiness has nothing to do with pleasure and pain. And this harmony you talk about, I regard it as a natural state with regards to me.

RAMESH So what is the happiness which God intended you to have?

Daniel It's exactly this harmony where I can trust the other person...

Ramesh So why have you distrusted that person? Why has no human being – except the very, very few exceptions who say 'Yes, I am happy'; 'I am enlightened' – been able to change this? I pursued this, and then the most important conclusion I came to is that the happiness I am seeking depending upon the harmonious relationship with the other – I did get it – and that itself is enlightenment!

In other words, enlightenment means having my real nature, reaching my real nature. And my real nature is happiness. That is the conclusion I came to; but at that point of time, I decided that God never intended any human being to be happy.

Tell me, could you have reached any other conclusion? Tell me.

Daniel Yes.

Ramesh Tell me.

Daniel As a human being, I have the capacity to live harmoniously with the other...

Ramesh Have you had it?

Daniel At certain times.

Ramesh So if you have had the capacity, why have you not been able to have a harmonious relationship with the other without the suspicion and fear?

Daniel Sometimes.

Ramesh Sometimes is not the point. Everytime! Sometimes is something everybody experiences. Sometimes everyone has done it.

DANIEL Hmm...

RAMESH But unless you are ready to do it everytime, you cannot be happy.

DANIEL So how is that...

RAMESH Aah! Therefore I decided that it is not possible. It is possible to do it sometimes, but not everytime. Therefore I decided God never intended man to be happy. And therefore the maximum happiness is to accept the pleasure and pain that has happened including the shattering of the pleasure and the intensification of the pain.

And I had totally accepted it. Not with resentment. That is the way it is supposed to be according to God's Will.

Therefore I accepted this without any resentment, as a fact of life, with total humility knowing that there is nothing I can do about it. And then when I had totally surrendered my pursuit of happiness, I got the answer from outside.

What do I mean by "answer from the outside"? The answer did not come to me from my intellect nor from my heart. The 'outside' can only mean God or the Source. The answer came to me in specific terms. "You are wrong. My intention has never been to make the human being unhappy. On the contrary, my intention for the human being was that it should be their birthright to be happy. But that birthright depended only on one factor and the human being has not accepted that factor. The human being has rejected that factor. And that is why the human being is unhappy. And the cruel joke is that, that one factor is the basis of every religion."

This is the answer I got. I repeat, "It is always been my intention that happiness be the birthright of every human being and that has depended on one factor but the human being has rejected that one factor."

Earlier I had considered that question. Why have there been so many religious wars? Can there not be one basis for all religions so that religious wars do not happen? The very fact that so many religious wars have happened can only mean that there cannot be one basis of every religion. But now my answer from God is, "There is one basis for all religions but the human being has rejected it!" So my next step was quite clear.

From that basis, with the total acceptance that happiness does not depend on the flow of life but on my attitude towards the other, I asked myself, "What is the basis of every religion?" And then I came across four beautiful words from the Bible, which I had come across so many times, almost twenty or thirty times. And those four words are: 'Thy Will be done'. Daniel, do you know those words? Do you believe in those words? What do they mean?

They don't need any interpretation. Do you know what Advaita Vedanta said? This is fullness and if you take away some, the fullness remains. You add fullness to it and the same fullness remains. That's not easy to understand, is it?

And that is what the Source says and that is in Advaita. But the Bible says – the Advaita is not concerned with daily living though I use the Advaita for daily living – 'Thy will be done'. I honestly cannot imagine four words which are simpler to understand. For me it is so clear. What it means is 'Thy Will be done'. It means that no one else's Will be done. Thy Will be done, therefore mine will not be done. Necessarily, which means nothing can happen unless it is God's Will.

Isn't that right? Thy Will be done which means nothing can happen unless it is God's Will. And I added 'Cosmic Law' for those who don't like the idea of a God. Now that is another interesting point. If I say 'Thy Will be done' to an atheist and tell him that nothing can happen unless God wills it to happen, the aethist will tell me "Ramesh, please do not talk to me about God. I don't believe in God."

Suppose an aethist tells me "I don't believe in God", what do you think my response will be?

DANIEL Call it something else.

RAMESH No, no. Whatever you call it, it is God!

DANIEL But you would say that to the atheist.

RAMESH My response would be "I agree with you." Do you know why? What is the basis on which the atheist says "I do not believe in God"?

I agree with him because the atheist says that what I am told, what my religion tells me, is that God is up there, an old man sitting there, with a big beard, keeping a track, by using a computer, of every sin which every human being does and waiting for him to finish his life and come to me and then I will punish him.

That idea or concept of God I am not prepared to accept and I say I will agree with him. What is the idea of God which 99 per cent of people have? What is the idea of God that you have? An entity, an all-powerful entity. Isn't that the idea you have? All-knowing, all-powerful entity. Whereas you and I are helpless entities. Whatever happens to us is because of what that entity does to us. Therefore we must pray to that all-powerful entity and say "Please, increase my pleasure and lessen my pain."

And that is what prayer means? Isn't it? Praying to the Almighty, the all-powerful God asking him to increase my pleasure and lessen my pain.

That is the God the atheist does not believe in, nor do I believe in.

What is the God I believe in? God is the Source. The One Unmanifest singularity, the one Unmanifest Oneness which has itself become the manifestation, the functioning of which is our daily living, the basis of which is duality.

The One Source has become the duality in manifestation. And this functioning we call life, beginning with male and female. The One Unmanifest has become the manifest duality, male and female and every conceivable duality – good and evil, beautiful and ugly, wealth and poverty, health and disease. Every kind of duality, interconnected opposites.

This means if you have one, you've got to have the other. You cannot have wealth without poverty. You cannot have health without disease. You cannot have a saint unless you have a psychopath. See what I mean?

Therefore my idea was the Source, One Source, which had become this. No human sitting on the throne, judging the human being. That is my idea of God! And nothing can happen unless it is the Will of God which means the One Singularity has become the manifest duality and whatever is supposed to happen has already been pre-determined.

The movie of life is already complete and in the can! We are witnessing the movie of life frame by frame by frame, whereas the movie is already in the can.

Therefore there is no God waiting to punish anybody. God knows that whatever has to happen will happen according to His Will, according to His script, the divine script. Everything has happened according to His divine script which is meant by 'Thy Will be done'. 'Thy Will be done' is the divine script.

Nothing can happen unless it is God's Will and Islam says the very same thing. The Hindu religion says the same thing in a more powerful way. Do you know what the Hindu religion says? The Bible says 'Thy Will be done'. The Hindu religion says 'Thou art the doer, thou art the experiencer'. Why? Because you are the only Reality. You are the one single Source.

"Thou art the doer, thou art the experiencer. Thou art the speaker, thou art the listener." It looks as if Ramesh speaks, Daniel listens. Daniel speaks, Ramesh listens. But if both of us were in deep sleep or sedated into unconsciousness, neither of us would be able to speak nor listen. Isn't that right? Therefore if we were sedated into unconsciousness, none of us would be talking and listening.

Then it is clear who is doing the talking and who is doing the listening. It means Consciousness as the Source or God is doing the talking through one instrument and listening through another instrument. Talking through that instrument, listening through this instrument.

And based on that, I had my concept on enlightenment. That is another point I came to. I was seeking enlightenment as if enlightenment was a certified event. Now I came to know that enlightenment can only be a concept. An individual concept, my concept of enlightenement.

What is my concept of enlightenment? Based on this, my concept of enlightenment means: "Everything in the world is a happening according to God's Will / Cosmic Law. How each happening affects whom, for better or for worse – a happening hurts someone or a happening helps someone – that also is according to God's Will / Cosmic Law. And through which body-mind instrument that happening happens, which the society calls my action or your action, his action or her action, is also according to God's Will / Cosmic Law.

No human being is capable of doing anything. Total acceptance of this concept is enlightenment."

My second question, which is more important: What will enlightenement do for me that I did not have before? And the answer is, the happiness that I get by accepting totally that I cannot be the doer nor can you be the doer means immediately, the total collapse of the load of guilt and shame which I have been carrying for the other and the bigger load of hatred for the other for their actions in hurting me.

The entire load of hatred, hatred for myself for hurting others and the much bigger load of hatred for others for their actions in hurting me – the entire load of hatred disappears. And that is the load of hatred which would be suffering, which had the power to shatter my pleasure in the moment or intensify my pain of the moment.

I am enjoying something now. Then, a memory of something I had done to hurt my father for which he has never forgiven me...a memory of that arises and my pleasure is shattered and my pain is intensified. Or something which a personal friend or my brother did to me, for which I have never really forgiven him...a memory of that incident has the power to increase or intensify my pain.

Once I am able to accept totally that the human being is incapable of doing anything, good or evil; once I am able to accept totally that a happening *happens* – whether it means good things for someone or bad things for the other is not in my control. I am merely an instrument through which a happening happens which the society calls my deed and for which the society rewards me or punishes me. Reward from the society means pleasure; punishment from the society means pain. And that is daily living.

So, as I was saying, I pursued enlightenment as the supreme happiness – which is the impression I had been given. I pursued enlightenment as the supreme achievement...which brought me frustration.

Now I know that that the happiness which I pursued is my very nature and that depends on my accepting totally that I cannot do anything to hurt anyone. No one can do anything to hurt me. We are all instruments through which the Source or Consciousness or Energy or God functions and brings about whatever is supposed to happen according to the Cosmic Law.

What is the basis of this? The human brain is incapable of knowing the basis. Why? Because the Cosmic Law concerns the entire universe for all times. The Universal or Cosmic Law does not concern only one planet in one solar system, among thousands of solar systems and six billion inhabitants on that planet.

Therefore what happens? 'Thy Will' or 'according to the Cosmic Law'. We cannot question it. We have to accept it. If you are able to accept it, that is enlightenment, that is happiness. That means the end of suffering. Suffering being that which intensifies the pain in the moment and shatters the pleasure in the moment. Okay, Daniel? So any questions?

DANIEL The question that comes up is that after knowing this...

RAMESH The only point is that the acceptance of this concept must be total.

DANIEL What is the practical way you suggest to totally accept? In our nature it is hard to totally accept and be totally devoted.

RAMESH So what you are saying is that Daniel is not sure whether his acceptance would ever be total?

DANIEL That's true.

RAMESH Daniel, intellectually, even a damn fool will accept this concept because this means the end of suffering.

DANIEL I have no problem accepting it intellectually.

RAMESH Aah! Therefore the question is how can my intellectual acceptance become total acceptance? Since you are not the doer, there is nothing you can do about it. Therefore it means that it will happen only if it is supposed to happen, according to the Cosmic Law and your destiny.

Then a valid question arises. While I am waiting for something to happen, while I am waiting for God to make up His mind, is there not something I can do for spiritual practice? Have you been doing some practices now? What have you been doing?

DANIEL Meditation and Yoga.

RAMESH So your question is that now, knowing that I can't do anything because I am not the doer, what do I do about the various spiritual practices I have been doing? Valid question, isn't it?

DANIEL It does not conflict with the practice, I think.

RAMESH Why? You are not the doer.

DANIEL I find my meditation practice enables me to surrender.

RAMESH So what you are saying is that your spiritual practices bring you pleasure.

DANIEL Not always.

RAMESH Not always? So when do your spiritual practices not bring you pleasure?

DANIEL They bring pleasure and pain. It's just being with whatever there is.

RAMESH When do your spiritual practices not bring you pain?

DANIEL Depends. If I am sitting for meditation and pleasure likewise.

RAMESH In other words, are you doing the spiritual practices because you feel you are forced to do them or you do them because you like doing them?

DANIEL I don't always like to do them. I feel it's something I am compelled to do.

RAMESH You are forced to do it, compelled to do it.

DANIEL Not compelled but...

RAMESH You used the word 'compel'...

DANIEL I don't know if 'compel' is the right word but it's something I do naturally, already.

RAMESH So my answer to that is simple. Whenever you feel like doing it because it gives you pleasure, do it. Whenever you feel, you would rather not do it, for whatever reason, don't do it. In a given situation, you have the total free will to do whatever you like.

DANIEL I feel that to get a sense of this total freedom, sometimes I need to, in a way, discipline my mind.

RAMESH The only thing to understand is that whatever spiritual practices you may do, they will not bring you the ultimate freedom because those are the practices which you are doing. And you cannot be the doer.

Therefore, for all the existing spiritual practices – do them if you like to do them; give them up if you don't like to do them. But then another question still remains. While I am waiting for God to make up His mind, is there not something which I can do to pass time? Because I am used to doing some spiritual practices with the understanding that that spiritual practice will have nothing to do with the ultimate result. Just to pass time. It is a valid question.

And for that I do have a suggestion which I call personal investigation. Very, very simple matter because you are not really doing anything. If you find the time to do it during the day, you are free to do it any day. But if you don't find time during the day, then at the end of the day, take ten minutes off, sit quietly, and be comfortable. This is not a discipline. Take the most comfortable seat and have a glass of beer if that makes you more comfortable and do some very simple personal investigation. Personal investigation of a particular action which you are sure is your action.

If you go through the events of the day, you will come to the conclusion that most of the events were happening over which you had no control and you were only a part of the happening. So from those events, choose one event, one action, which Daniel is sure is my action. Others I do not know, but this one is my action. And then investigate it. The investigation is simple.

If I consider this particular action as my action, then, did I decide to do that action at a particular time? And then you will realize "No, I didn't". And then you will realise that if I did not decide to do it then how did the action happen? And then you will remember that you had a thought and that thought led to your action. If that thought would not have happened, your action would not have happened. You had no control over the happening of that thought because no one can have any control over what the next thought is going to be. No one can know what the next thought is going to be.

It comes from the Source or God or Consciousness. If that thought would not have happened, your action would not have happened. And you had no control over that thought. How can you call that action your action? You have done the investigation yourself and come to the conclusion that the one action you were sure was your action turns out, from your own investigation, to be not your action, then your acceptance must go considerably deeper.

And I can assure you that you can investigate any number of actions, and every single time, without exception, you will keep coming to the conclusion "not my action", "not my action", and each time your acceptance will go deeper and deeper. If I had not happened to be at a certain place or time and seen something, my action would not have happened. And I had no control at being at that time, at that place. And much more important, but for some happening, which I happened to see, or hear, or smell, or taste, or touch, my action would not have happened. How can I call it my action? And each time the understanding goes deeper and deeper until at a particular moment of time, if is your destiny, God's Will / Cosmic Law, a divine flash is likely to happen: "I simply cannot be the doer."

And once that divine flash happens, there will be no more doubt that neither you are the doer nor anyone else is the doer. And then there is no more doubt and your acceptance will be total.

Okay, Daniel? So, if during the day any questions arise, you are free to come again and we will deal with them. If there are any questions or doubts or even comments, we will deal with them. Are you likely to be here for a few more days?

DANIEL Yes, three or four more days.

RAMESH So come again and we will deal with them, whether they are questions or comments.

$\mathcal{Y}_{\partial}$

FOUR

'Happiness *is* Enlightenment!'

ℛ

RAMESH You want to interview me? What is the basis of the interview? What is it called? Is it part of something bigger?

TIYAMARA It is! It is part of a television series of inspiring individuals in the world, who are contributing to humanity.

RAMESH I see.

TIYAMARA And so the reason to interview you is that you have an understanding that contributes to humanity. That's why people want to come and listen to you.

RAMESH I see, I see. But you know, people here, I mean this place here, can accommodate a maximum of hundred people and what I usually have are about 25 to 30 people.

TIYAMARA Yes.

RAMESH You know that?

TIYAMARA I know that.

RAMESH I am not the person who inspires hundreds of people. Let us be clear about that.

TIYAMARA Well, you will inspire hundreds of people when they watch you and listen to you on television. You have the capacity for that. So...

RAMESH Anyway, this is part of...what I mean is, you want to interview several people and make...

TIYAMARA A series, a total series.

RAMESH I see, I understand...any particular subject for this series?

TIYAMARA Well, it's really exploring...it's different for different people because...

RAMESH I know, I know, but it's bound to have a title, surely?

TIYAMARA A title? The title of it is 'Inspiring Lives'. So, it is very general. What we are looking at is – what is it that people can learn...

RAMESH What's the title? Could you please repeat that? The title is...

TIYAMARA 'Inspiring Lives'.

RAMESH Inspiring...Lives...I see, I see, 'Inspiring Lives'!

TIYAMARA That's right! And so we are talking with inspiring individuals about content that can contribute to people when they are journeying through life.

Ramesh Forgive my interfering, but at the moment how many people have you interviewed, so far?

Tiyamara We have just started today. Well, we started actually with a gentleman on Saturday and now...

Ramesh I see. So I am the number two in this series...

Tiyamara You are! May be, mixed around later, in terms of the order.

Ramesh I see. Are you sure that the others you are going to interview won't feel jealous?

Tiyamara Oh, they might be!

Ramesh Or you would rather want them to be?

Tiyamara It doesn't really matter anyway, does it? (*Laughs.*)

Ramesh Tiyamara, that's an interesting point. It doesn't matter, you see! It doesn't matter to whom, Tiyamara? It doesn't matter to whom?

Tiyamara It doesn't matter in the cosmic plan of it all.

Ramesh I see, I see. So now, on this point, the title is 'Inspiring Lives'. I go again and again, because whatever we talk about, we must never forget the title of your series, 'Inspiring Lives'.

Tiyamara Right, okay.

Ramesh That's why I am interested in the title, otherwise what is likely to happen is we go off the mark in all kinds of things and forget this – the main purpose – 'Inspiring Lives'.

Tiyamara Okay. Now, as a subtext to that I would say that part of the angle of the series is to explore ideas and content and experiences of the people who have led inspiring lives, that actually can contribute to other people leading their lives in a way that is better for them. So it's about people being able to grow in some way from the content.

Ramesh So, the point is, to inspire people to live their lives in a particular way?

Tiyamara Perhaps!

Ramesh What is the inspiration about? What I mean is...I want to get the base clear. 'Inspiring Lives'...What am I supposed to be doing to inspire people, to do what?

Tiyamara Okay. So, there are two aspects to that. One is that inspiring people to create a better life for themselves...

Ramesh Wait a minute. Could you repeat that please?

Tiyamara Inspiring people to create a better life for themselves. So that people can live in a way...I guess...get more happiness for themselves.

Ramesh Aah, now, I agree somewhere!

Tiyamara Yeah, more happiness. And particularly in relation to themselves, in the world, into their life; so their relationship is in a happier way, in a way that is more expansive or freer. And the other aspect we are looking at in the series is the fact that people can contribute somehow towards humanity or society in some way. So, these are two kinds of angles.

Ramesh I see, I see. On this point, let me be perfectly clear that whatever I say, is going to inspire the individual to be happier for himself. See, what I mean? I make it clear because whatever I say, the intention is not to make a happier world, I want to be clear on that. You see what I mean?

Tiyamara Yes, I do.

Ramesh There may be people, who consider that their lives are meant to make the world a happier place, I am not one of those.

Tiyamara No?

Ramesh That is what I want to make perfectly clear.

Tiyamara So you are saying that you are more about the individual living from a place of more happiness.

Ramesh What I am concerned with, is to inspire the individual to be more happy in this life, himself. That is the point.

Tiyamara Yeah, in doing that, does that not have an impact on the world, if we have more individuals inspired to lead a happier life?

Ramesh Therefore what you are saying is, in my telling any individual how to be happier than he is now, how to be really happy, it may affect the outer world.

Tiyamara That's right!

Ramesh But my point is, it may or it may not. So what I want to make again and again perfectly clear is, that I do not consider it my responsibility to contribute to the happiness of the world. That is God's business and I leave it to God.

TIYAMARA So, do you consider it your responsibility to contribute to the happiness of individuals or is it simply that it's a movement and joy and you need to do that?

RAMESH Now, that's a very good question. And the answer is, I do not think, Tiyamara, I have any responsibility whatsoever towards anybody and that is the basis of my happiness!

TIYAMARA Well, that was one of my questions about responsibility. So does the individual have any responsibility for anything?

RAMESH That is the point! One of the main reasons for the unhappiness of the individual human being, according to me, is that he considers himself to be in control of his life, one, and two, he has the responsibility to live a life in such a way that it inspires others to be good people. See what I mean? Whereas the basis of my total conviction is, that everything happens according to God's Will. We can say according to God's Will or we can say according to Cosmic Law, I have no preference.

TIYAMARA So, is there any way that you can serve God's Will or do you just do whatever you like, whenever you want, and God's Will occurs... can you serve God's Will?

RAMESH Very good question, Tiyamara, very good question. Therefore the reason I say, most importantly, that I don't think I have the slightest responsibility either towards myself or towards the other. I honestly don't think I have any responsibility either towards myself or to my family or towards the society in general. That is because, according to my concept, every human being, fundamentally, is a three dimensional object...

What is the manifestation? Manifestation is the totality of all three dimensional objects of various kinds. What are the various kinds? First, there is the stone in which there is no apparent life; so we call the stone, an inanimate thing. Second, there is the growing plant which grows by itself, no need to water it. Therefore there is life in the growing plant. Third, there is the animal in which the three dimensional object has five senses through which the individual animal is able to see, hear, smell, taste and touch. In the case of a growing plant, there is no sense of any individuality; in the animal, there is a distinct sense of being a separate entity who is concerned with his own happiness. Therefore the animal is a three dimensional object in which there are five senses through which the separate entity is able to see, hear, smell, taste or touch; and the separate entity is what I call the 'ego'. The three dimensional object is part of manifestation, and the 'ego' – the sense of identification as a separate entity – can therefore only be concerned with the Unmanifest Source. This feeling of being a separate entity which I call the 'ego' – is connected with the Source. In other words, the Source, the Unmanifest Oneness, the Unmanifest Singularity has become the manifest duality.

TIYAMARA O.K. So the ego is connected to the Source?

RAMESH Yes, what I am trying to say is, that according to my concept, God did not create this world. The Unmanifest Singularity, Oneness, the Unmanifest Unicity, had to become the two in the manifestation. Why? Because the basis of manifestation is duality, beginning with male and female, and the other dualities of every conceivable kind. So, the Unmanifest Oneness had to become manifest duality. Duality, beginning with male and female and duality of every conceivable kind like wealth and poverty, health and disease, goodness and evil, saint and psychopath, generous man and a miser. Therefore, the Source, the Singularity, the Unmanifest itself has become the manifestation.

TIYAMARA The purpose of that is...

RAMESH Aah, the purpose of it! The point is, for me, that there is no purpose. Then why did the manifestation get created? Isn't that your question?

TIYAMARA Yes.

RAMESH If there is no purpose, then why did the Creator create the manifestation? That is the question that must prevail if you say that God created the world. But my point is, the one Unmanifest Source was forced to become the manifested duality. Why?

TIYAMARA Forced by...

RAMESH Forced by its own nature! Therefore there is no question of purpose for creating the world! There would be a purpose in creating the world if we think in terms of a God creating the world. Then the natural question, valid question, will be: why does God have to create the world and make people suffer? Could he not sit quietly or sleep quietly without bothering to create the world and people who are unhappy? And it is a valid question, isn't it? But the question cannot arise on the basis of my concept that there is no God who created the world. The one Unmanifest Singularity itself was forced to become the manifest duality.

TIYAMARA By its own nature?

RAMESH By its own nature! So, what is this nature, which forces the Unmanifest Unicity into becoming duality? My concept therefore is, the Source has to be potential energy – dead matter cannot create anything.

TIYAMARA Right.

RAMESH Therefore, my point is – if I consider, conceive of the Unmanifested Singularity as potential energy, throbbing potential energy, then it is in the nature of potential energy to activise itself sometime, otherwise, it will be dead matter. Therefore the throbbing potential energy was forced to activise itself sometime and then there was the Big Bang and the manifestation.

TIYAMARA So, back to my question, can an individual serve the... cosmic play or...

RAMESH Now, you are saying, can the individual do something? And my point is – what is the individual that we are talking about? Earlier we came to the animal which is a three dimensional body-mind organism with a separate sense of an individual. Finally, there is the human being. Finally the fourth type of object is the human being, in which there is life, there is the body-mind instrument, five senses through which the separate entity is able to see, hear, smell, taste and touch and in the ego of the human being has been infused the sense of personal doership and intellect. The animal's ego doesn't have the intellect; it doesn't bother who feeds it so long as it is fed. The human being has the intellect which makes him ask the questions that you are asking...

TIYAMARA Right.

RAMESH So, the human being is fundamentally a three dimensional object in which life has been infused by the Source, along with various other infusions which makes him ask the questions. But fundamentally, every human being is a three dimensional object.

TIYAMARA Okay. So the search for purpose is somehow related to the sense of unhappiness, in duality, is that right?

RAMESH Therefore, what is the purpose of life? My answer is, according to me, the meaning and purpose of life for any individual is to be happy. That is all. All he wants is to be happy.

Tiyamara So, in many, many cases, an individual, in order to feel happy, seeks purpose, and if I am hearing you right, then you are saying, fundamentally, that there is no purpose. There is only a caused manifestation.

Ramesh This individual entity, the 'ego', which is the Source, the Impersonal Consciousness identified with each human body-mind organism as a separate entity with a sense of personal doership and intellect. So, every human being is fundamentally a three dimensional object with an ego who is identified with that body-mind organism.

Tiyamara Okay. So, really are you saying that the purpose is simply to be happy?

Ramesh Yes. So, my point therefore is, as soon as the newborn baby seeks its mother's breasts intuitively, all that the human being wants, according to my concept is – Happiness. The human being individually has nothing to do with the happiness of the world. That's what the intellect, the human intellect brings about and makes him unhappy.

Tiyamara Can one individual serve the process of happiness in another individual? It's a realization basically, isn't it...?

Ramesh Wait a minute, wait a minute...Now, whatever our purpose in life, what we are saying is therefore, what does the human being has to do in order to be happy, isn't that right?

Tiyamara Yes.

Ramesh But the most important point I am making is that the human being is fundamentally a three dimensional object through which the Source or the primal energy is functioning and bringing about whatever is supposed to happen according to God's Will or Cosmic Law.

TIYAMARA Can you say that again?

RAMESH Yes…What is the basis of manifestation? What is the manifestation? A collection of three dimensional objects, one kind of object being the human being who is a three dimensional object with which an ego is concerned as a separate entity with a sense of personal doership and intellect to ask the questions. Therefore, it is only the human being who asks, 'What am I here for?' That's what the question you have and the whole series of it. 'What am I here for?' And my direct answer to that is, 'You are here only for one simple purpose and that is, you want to be happy.'

Supposing you want to make the whole world happy and you succeeded in making the whole world happy, what will it do for you? You will be happy…you will be happy by being successful in making the world happy. Why is a generous man, a generous man? Because by being generous and helping others, makes him feel happy! Why is a miser, a miser? A miser is a miser because not being a miser and if forced to give money to help someone, makes him feel bad! In other words, a miser is happy if he is a miser and a generous man is happy if he is generous. Therefore, the miser did not choose to be a miser and the generous man did not choose to be a generous man! The saint did not choose to be a saint and a psychopath did not choose to be a psychopath! Therefore, the generous man and the miser, the saint and the psychopath are a typical example of the basic duality of manifestation and its functioning that we call 'Life'.

Therefore, my most important concept is that the human being can fundamentally only be a three dimensional object and a three dimensional object cannot do anything, let alone think whether what he is doing is right or wrong. Therefore, my fundamental basic concept is that every human being is a three dimensional object through which the Source or God or Impersonal Consciousness or pure energy functions and brings about whatever is supposed to happen according to God's Will or a Cosmic Law.

TIYAMARA In relation to this, this is the functional working mind that you talk about which helps us function on daily, worldly role...

RAMESH So, you are talking of the mind without which the human being will not be able to live his daily life.

TIYAMARA That's right. And then it is the thinking mind which is the culprit!

RAMESH Quite right! I am surprised that you thought about this working mind and thinking mind. You must have read...

TIYAMARA Oh, I read you. I read your book.

RAMESH In fact that is one of my concepts which you won't find elsewhere, I don't think so.

TIYAMARA Right, yeah...In relation to that, when you are dealing with other individuals, then you use your working mind to decide whether an individual is trustworthy or...

RAMESH Indeed, indeed!

TIYAMARA So, you use your discernment, which is your working mind, and then once you have made a choice, then you can be trusting, right? Because everything else is...

RAMESH I tell you what. I will bring you to one sentence which will tell you the whole story.

TIYAMARA Okay.

RAMESH And that is, what is the human being seeking? Happiness! And therefore I say whatever people may call enlightenment, for me enlightenment means being happy. I may shock millions of people, but that is my honest opinion. When people are trying to get enlightenment, my point is what they are really trying to get is happiness for themselves. Why? Because happiness is the very nature of the human being. Happiness is the nature of the human being, that's why right from the moment the newborn baby seeks its mother's breast intuitively, what the human being is seeking is happiness for himself. See what I mean? But the intellect takes him away...by giving him a wrong impression about what is happiness! Basically, the human being wants happiness and for the newborn baby, mother's milk is happiness.

TIYAMARA So how come you are saying that there is the non doing when you create space I suppose...to having the working mind mechanism going...

RAMESH Now, wait a minute. You are telling me that I create space... (*Laughter.*)

TIYAMARA Well, I don't know what you are doing. You were saying in your book that the thinking mind causes the problem.

RAMESH Therefore, Tiyamara, do you have limited time in which you have to do this job?

TIYAMARA Today or when?

RAMESH Otherwise what I am saying is let us go step by step, so that we don't get confused.

TIYAMARA Okay.

RAMESH So, step by step. Now, again, my basic thing is – whatever the philosophers may say, as far as I am concerned, the meaning and purpose of life for every human being is to be happy. Why? Because, happiness is our very own nature. So, what happens thereafter? Only question thereafter is, what truly is the happiness that I am seeking? What truly is happiness which is my real nature? That is the question. Now, the baby grows into the child. For the school going child, Tiyamara, what is happiness? Happiness means parents' love at home, success in the classroom, success on the playing field. That is happiness. The schoolboy is not concerned with anything else. Schoolboy grows into an adult and the adult is enticed by the various pleasures in life. Therefore, every adult pursues various pleasures in life with the mistaken notion that he is pursuing happiness.

Most of the people do not get the pleasures they want. They live a frustrated life, and they die a frustrated death. On what basis? On the basis of the Cosmic Law! The Bible says, 'Thy Will be done'. Nothing can happen unless it is the Will of God. I accept it, but for those who are not concerned with God I would say, nothing can happen or nothing really has happened unless it's according to a Cosmic Law, the basis of which a human brain is incapable of knowing anything because the Cosmic Law concerns the entire universe, for all the time; something so vast and complex, the human brain cannot understand. Therefore my basic concept is, whatever happens, whatever has been happening in the world at any time, whatever is happening now and whatever is going to happen in future is precisely according to the Cosmic Law.

TIYAMARA So, the impulse in an individual to do anything, is that therefore, a cosmic impulse?

RAMESH Therefore, that impulse can only arise on the basis of what is infused in that body-mind organism. In different human body-mind organisms, different infusions have been infused by the Creator and therefore, in a given situation, different impulses arise in different body-mind organisms. The impulse is not always the same.

TIYAMARA So, we…

RAMESH Now, therefore, I said, let us proceed step by step. We came to a stage where I said – the adult is unhappy, he lives a frustrated life, he dies a frustrated death because he pursues pleasure with the mistaken notion that he is pursuing happiness and why should that be so? My answer is, according to the Cosmic Law, the basis of which my brain is incapable of knowing. But among those who have been pursuing pleasure, a select few – And who does the selection? According to the Cosmic Law! – certain few people like us, who the world calls spiritual seekers, those few of us want enlightenment. Why do we want enlightenment? Because we expect enlightenment to make us happy. Therefore when we seek enlightenment, my point is, whether you realize it or not, when anybody seeks enlightenment, what he is really seeking is happiness for himself, not for the world. See what I mean?

Therefore, the most important conclusion I come to, which will be totally different from the conclusions you will come across from others, is that pursuing enlightenment is pursuing happiness for yourself. Why? Because happiness is our very nature. So, some of us realize – "I am seeking happiness." And who am I? By the grace of God I am someone who is reasonably comfortable in life over which I have no control, for which I can only be grateful to the Creator, and I am someone who has the common sense to know that the very basis of life is uncertainty.

The very basis of life is, every human being from the beginning of time has had the total free will to do whatever he or she feels like doing in a given situation, from the beginning of time. That is the fact, the basic fact number one. Every human being has the total free will to do whatever he or she wants at any given time and yet nobody knows whether what he has done will bring him pleasure or pain. Two basic facts of life: basic fact number one, every human being has had the total free will to do whatever he or she wants in any given situation; and the basic fact number two is, no one has ever had any control over the result and consequences of his action.

The basic conclusion from these two basic facts of life is that the human being certainly does have free will because without free will the mechanism of daily living would not have happened. What is the basic mechanism of daily living? Every human being, at every place and every time, has just done whatever he or she has felt like doing and daily living has started! Therefore, for the mechanism of daily living to happen, God was forced to give the human being total free will to do whatever he wanted in any given situation. The basic fact number two, no one has had any control over the result and consequences of his action, which is what it leads to, either the pleasure in the moment or the pain in the moment. Therefore these two basic facts lead to only one conclusion and that is, the human being does have total free will, but it is worthless in practice.

TIYAMARA Given what you have said, then truth is, people may think it's their free will, but it's really by conditioning and genes, of what they think is right or wrong and good or bad and...

RAMESH Quite right! Therefore, Tiyamara, I asked myself what is the basis on which I make decision of what to do? And the conclusion I came to was – that at any time, the decision I make depends only on two factors. Not two hundred factors, not even a third factor, only two factors: my genes and my up-to-date conditioning. I have no control over being born to particular parents, therefore I have no control over the genes in this human object. And more and more research is bringing out, how powerful this factor of genes is! You must have read it in the paper, more and more research is going on into genes and they are coming to very strange conclusions.

TIYAMARA And then the conditioning, which you can impact...

Ramesh No, no, I haven't come to the conditioning yet, I am still with genes…

Tiyamara Okay.

Ramesh So, what I am saying is that recently, in the last six months, I read about the results of research, of responsible research, not any… you see, people call it research but you know what they do, they do research in order to justify their conclusion and that's not research. But even responsible research has come to the conclusion that whether I am a generous person or not depends on my genes. Whether I am a despot in life, doing whatever I want to do, pressurising others to do whatever I want them to do or whether I am a victim of such a person, depends on my genes.

Tiyamara How does that follow if you have distinctly different generations? Like you know, like you have maybe parents who are very generous and children who are very selfish?

Ramesh So, whatever it is, my parents, grandparents or maybe ten generations back, so what your genes are based on, no one can know, all that the research has said is whether I am generous or not depends on my genes and whether I am a powerful, forceful character or a laid-back one, whether I am a bully or timid, depends on genes. And do you know the most astonishing thing I have read? Whether I am faithful to my wife or not depends on my genes. Mind you, that's from responsible research! Therefore, genes are such a powerful factor. Almost anything I do or think can be traced to some gene. Research, which has already been done! God knows what further research is going to bring about!

Tiyamara So, you are suggesting, in that case, that you can't rehabilitate someone or grow and change…

Ramesh So, therefore, the other factor is conditioning. Just as I had no control over being born to particular parents and therefore no control over my genes, which is such a powerful factor, similarly, I have no control over being born to particular parents in a particular geographical environment, in the particular social environment: upper class, upper middle class, lower or low class. In which environment this body-mind organism has received its conditioning from day one – the conditioning at home, the way my parents and other relatives behave, conditioning in the relevant society, how people in that society behave, conditioning in the school and/or college in that relevant society and conditioning in church or temple.

A bombardment of conditioning from day one: this is good and that is bad, you must do this and you must not do that, this is socially acceptable and that is socially not acceptable, this is a sin and God will punish you. Therefore, my point is, whatever I do at any moment consciously as my decision, it subconsciously depends entirely on these two factors, my genes and my conditioning. Genes, more or less stable, so far, anyway, but conditioning keeps on changing all the time.

TIYAMARA And you can choose how you can change your conditioning. How you expose yourself to...

RAMESH Anything you read or hear or experience can change your existing conditioning. What is happening now, let me be clear, is fresh conditioning. I am conveying to you my concept which can amend or alter your existing conditioning or even transform it.

TIYAMARA So, in terms of conditioning, obviously that is one thing we can use as our free will to impact.

RAMESH Indeed!

TIYAMARA And am I right in understanding that even though we may choose to condition ourselves in a particular way, well, I mean even in schools, I condition my children in a particular way or parents condition their children...

RAMESH You are free to improve yourself, any way you want.

TIYAMARA That's right and it's not equal to...happiness? It's about pleasure? Maybe...or maybe not?

RAMESH Wait a minute. Now we are talking about daily living. Now we are talking about the mechanism of daily living. Mechanism of daily living, means – I do whatever I feel like doing at any moment but on analysis I find that whatever I have been doing is based on two factors, my genes and my up-to-date conditioning, over neither of which have I had any control.

TIYAMARA Oh! You can have some control over your up-to-date conditioning, surely, because you can choose what input you...

RAMESH That you are talking about improvement, self improvement. So, about self improvement, again, at any moment I am free to improve myself physically, mentally, temperamentally, spiritually, financially, any way I want, I have the total free will. But the point is having done whatever I think I should do, the result is never ever in my control and which is what the human being forgets.

TIYAMARA Yes...Oh, well we can have the impact on the...

RAMESH And the result, the success or the partial success or failure has an impact on what we do next. Therefore you are free to improve yourself but to what extent you can improve yourself is not in your control. Therefore, whatever one has done at any moment as one's free will, turns out on inspection to be something which one has been forced to do by his or her own genes or up-to-date conditioning.

Therefore, the conclusion I come to, which is the basis of my happiness, the basic conclusion I come to is – in order to live my daily life, I am forced to do whatever I want and I go and do it but having done it, where does my happiness lie? I repeat, in any given situation, like anybody else I do precisely what I feel like doing, knowing that it is really not my doing because what I have been doing is based on two factors, my genes and my conditioning, which God has infused in this body-mind organism. Therefore, any action which I know I have done and which the society considers as my action is based on two factors over neither of which have I had any control. Who has control over these? God, the Creator has! He has infused these two conditions, my genes and my up-to-date conditioning because of which I have just done something.

With that total acceptance – whatever I have been doing all my life is based on two factors which God infused in this body-mind organism – the mind boggling conclusion I come to, Tiyamara, is – in daily living, I cannot make a mistake because whatever I have done is precisely what God expected me to do. Whatever I have done is based on two factors which God infused in this body-mind organism, therefore, whether the society considers it as a mistake and punishes me and the punishment leads to pain in the moment, I know that it was not a mistake and that is precisely what I was supposed to do. Much, much more importantly, Tiyamara, I know that I cannot commit a sin. Whatever has happened through this body-mind organism, which the society considers my action, God does not consider it a sin because whatever I have been doing is precisely what God expected me to do. More accurately, whatever I have been doing is precisely what God has been doing through this three dimensional object which the society has been considering as my actions.

TIYAMARA So, that brings me back to my original question, which was, 'Can an individual serve God?' That the impulse in an individual to do anything is caused by...

Ramesh Sent by God! Yes!

Tiyamara That's right. So even if you have an impulse to serve, that comes, it is not from yourself...

Ramesh Therefore, I cannot commit a sin whatever the society may do to me. The psychopath and the criminal cannot commit a sin, irrespective of whatever the society may do to them!

Tiyamara So, that's the judgment of the society, not...

Ramesh Not in my control! Therefore, if the society's judgment brings me pleasure, I enjoy it and if the society's judgment brings me pain, I suffer it. I have no choice but I don't take any pride if there is pleasure, and I don't condemn myself as having done something wrong if there is pain! Pleasure and pain, according to Cosmic Law, which I have to enjoy or suffer, but I commit no sin and I don't have to worry about God punishing me.

Tiyamara So, in your perception, where does the world of self-improvement sit?

Ramesh I told you! Every human being is free to improve himself or herself physically, mentally, temperamentally, spiritually or financially, anyway she wants. She can take any course, positive thinking or whatever, nobody stops her. If she has the money to take any course, she will take the course but having taken the course, what success she will achieve has never ever been in her control.

Tiyamara But when I spoke to you the last time you did say that you can increase the percentage of a certain outcome. You can't guarantee but you can increase the percentage, we spoke about that!

Ramesh No, how much percentage there will be improvement or not is not in your control, anyway. Whether there will be improvement or not is not in your control. How much percentage of improvement or no improvement at all... again, not in your control!

TIYAMARA From an energy point of view though, we are all energy bodies as it were and so...can we not choose to use our mind...

RAMESH You can choose anything you want!

TIYAMARA Yes, and have an impact!

RAMESH I am sorry...?

TIYAMARA And have an impact so that...

RAMESH Yes, but the only thing that you don't know is, the result and the consequences of that impact. That's the whole point. Therefore, my whole basic concept is: the human being is fundamentally a three dimensional object...

TIYAMARA So, for example, did you hear about when they said that there was a group of Buddhist monks and they all meditated in New York and the crime rate went down. Did you hear that story?

RAMESH Oh, yes, indeed! Indeed, it did happen.

TIYAMARA So, therefore, they had chosen...

RAMESH No, no, wait a minute. Therefore, what was described, Tiyamara, was the mechanism of what happened, the mechanism of what happened. Another group of Buddhists comes and does like that; the improvement may not be the same. What was described is the mechanism of what happened.

Now, what happens is, my basic concept, I repeat – every human being is a machine, the basis of which is genes and up-to-date conditioning; that machine through which the Source functions or the primal energy as the Source functions and brings about whatever is supposed to happen according to a Cosmic Law, the basis of which the human brain is incapable of ever understanding. Therefore, we can only accept whatever happens as something which was precisely supposed to happen, precisely the way it has.

TIYAMARA So, your understanding...how does it serve happiness in people?

RAMESH So, the happiness I have is the same as what I call enlightenment. Which is the total acceptance of my concept that: Everything in the world is a happening, according to the Cosmic Law; how each happening affects whom, for better or worse – a happening happens, it may hurt me and help you or hurt you and help me – is again according to a Cosmic Law; through which body-mind organism or through which person, the happening happens which the society calls my action, your action or his action, is again, according to a Cosmic Law; the human being is incapable of doing anything. The total acceptance of that concept means enlightenment. That's my concept of enlightenment.

In other words, what I am telling you, which is the most important thing I can tell you, is that enlightenment or Self-realization or being one with God is not a certified event. Enlightenment or Self-realization or whatever you call it, is not a certified event. And unfortunately, people don't realize it.

According to me, enlightenment is a personal concept and I consider I am enlightened because I am happy. I am enlightened because I have got the happiness I am seeking. And the happiness I am seeking has nothing to do with the pleasures of life. Therefore, the quest for happiness...For the baby – mother's milk is happiness. For the child

– success in the classroom, success in the playing field and love from parents. For the adult – happiness means the total acceptance that he is incapable of doing anything. He is incapable of hurting anyone and no one is capable of hurting him, and the total acceptance of this means happiness.

And what is the basis of unhappiness? According to my concept the basis of unhappiness is – hatred. Condemning and hating myself for my actions, condemning and hating others for their actions is the suffering which prevents the human being from being happy. Therefore, for me, my concept – what is enlightenment? Enlightenment is happiness which is my true nature, that's why I am seeking enlightenment. And the happiness I am seeking I have got because I have been able to accept totally that I don't have to fear the other hurting me – not in his control; and I am not capable of hurting anyone – not in my control.

TIYAMARA So that means really that you can live in a place of complete trust. Like, we are all always protecting ourselves from being hurt or whatever...the bad stuff, what we perceive as bad stuff.

RAMESH But don't forget that the very mechanism of daily living is based on my doing in any situation, whatever I think I should do. Accepting that I am not the doer does not take away my birthright of total free will to do whatever I want in a given situation. But the important point we forget is that the result has never been in our control. Therefore, if I ask – and you could ask that to others in your interviews if you are talking about enlightenment – what is the one factor which blocks enlightenment? According to my concept, the one factor that blocks enlightenment is my conviction that I am in control of my life. I am in control of my life, I am responsible for what I do and therefore I bear an enormous burden of condemnation and hatred for myself for my actions and a much bigger load of condemnation and hatred for others for their action. And it is this load based on the total conviction that every human being is responsible for his actions, once that is removed, once this total conviction that I am the doer is removed, then, no more hating myself for my actions, no more hating others for their actions. And the absence of hatred is the basis of the happiness which I have got which is my very nature.

TIYAMARA So, that's something that you have come to yourself?

RAMESH You mean this conclusion?

TIYAMARA Yes?

RAMESH Yes, that's the conclusion I have come to myself...

TIYAMARA When did you start seeking?

RAMESH Aah! That's a good question. You want to know the answer? The answer is, Tiyamara, I pursued enlightenment for forty years and ended up in total frustration because all I wanted was answers to my two basic, valid questions: One, what precisely am I seeking or what is enlightenment? I was introduced to a guru, the guru gave me initiation, did something and said "Now I am your guru and you are my disciple." So, my first question was, what precisely is this enlightenment, which I am supposed to seek as the most important thing in life? Nobody could tell me. Why can no one tell you what is enlightenment? Because enlightenment is not a certified event. God has not certified any event as enlightenment. Therefore, what is enlightenment? No one can give you an answer and therefore my answer is – enlightenment is a concept and according to my concept you are enlightened if you are happy. If you have got the happiness you are seeking, you are enlightened.

My second question was: I am supposed to seek enlightenment, what will enlightenment do for me in case I do get this enlightenment? What happiness will I get after enlightenment that I didn't have before? No one could get me the answer. So, I once asked this question to my first guru and do you know he got angry that I dare to ask this question! Because he thought by asking that question, I was doubting his being enlightened. Then he realized when he looked around that I dared to ask this question because there were very few people, only five to six people, may be seven or eight. So, he got angry. But when he looked around, he saw everyone waiting for the answer. Everyone was waiting for the answer to "What will enlightenment do for me?" So, he calmed down and gave me an answer. You know what the answer was? The answer was: "You can only know when you are enlightened!" Now, I will say, "No, wrong! I can tell you what enlightenment will do for you. One, enlightenment will not give you any kind of bliss because according to me, bliss would still be an intense pleasure in life. Therefore, all I can tell you is the happiness, which is our real nature, is based not on anything positive in life, but the happiness means the end of suffering." And curiously I came to know later, this is what the Buddha has said, "Enlightenment means the end of suffering." And what is the suffering? The load of hatred for myself and hatred for the other, that is the suffering which ends, that is all.

Now, do you have any question?

TIYAMARA So, one of the things you say is that a lot of our unhappiness is derived, I mean, you just said, from – 'hatred', but also from the thinking mind. It's like a sense of separation and there will always be this idea to protect us...

RAMESH Now, wait a minute, wait a minute. You got in a very important word called 'separation'. A very important word called 'separation'. What is your understanding about 'separation'? What most masters have told you and you will interview other people, they will confirm it: "Enlightenment means the end of separation", "Enlightenment means the end of ego" and that is something, Tiyamara, I simply could not accept for one reason. The greatest of the sages, Ramana Maharshi, for instance, even after the ultimate experience, still continued to live his life in the ashram for fifty years as the same separate entity. Therefore how can you say that "enlightenment means the end of separation."

Tiyamara   What do you mean by the same separate entity?

Ramesh   He still lived as a separate entity. If I had called him by name, 'Ramana' or 'Bhagwan' or whatever, would he not have turned and responded to my call? So if Ramana has responded to my calling him by name, is it not separation?

Tiyamara   I don't know, I guess, that depends, I would mention that those are functional aspects...maybe a   functionality that continues but...

Ramesh   I call Ramana by name and he responds and the basis of that response is – he is the one, whose name I called as a separate entity, otherwise he would not have responded.

Tiyamara   Yeah.

Ramesh   Therefore, I simply could not accept the "end of separation, end of ego" as the basis of enlightenment. I just could not accept it. Therefore, now, I have come to the conclusion; what is enlightenment? Enlightenment means the total acceptance that I am not the doer of my actions; the other is not the doer of his actions and every action is a happening brought about by the Source according to a Cosmic Law. Therefore, my question about the enlightenment is, if the sage continues to live as the same ego and the ordinary person also lives his life as an ego, a separate entity, what is the difference? See? And that difference is what I call enlightenment. And enlightenment means, according to my concept, in the ego of the sage, the sense of personal doership has been totally uprooted. So that Ramana Maharshi himself describes this fact by saying that "the ego of a sage is like remnants of a burnt rope."

TIYAMARA A burnt...?

RAMESH "The ego of a sage is like the remnants of a burnt rope."
When you hear that, what is the most important significance you attach
to this statement? I repeat, Ramana Maharshi, "the ego of a sage is like
remnants of a burnt rope." What do you say is the significance for you,
of that statement?

TIYAMARA The remnants...of a burnt rope...

RAMESH "Remnants of a burnt rope..." What is of significance here?
I give significance to the "ego" of the sage. Therefore, when Ramana
Maharshi describes the ego of a sage – whatever the description, that
can vary, the important fact is a sage like Ramana Maharshi admits
that even the sage has an ego. Therefore, to say that enlightenment
means the end of separation is stupid, nonsense. Someone said it and
others have kept parroting it. So, in my case, as I told you, because
my two questions had not been answered, I pursued enlightenment for
forty years and ended up in total frustration.

So, when I retired from work, I decided once and for all, no more
enlightenment for me. I don't care a damn what enlightenment is, so for
the rest of my life I will be a very selfish person and pursue happiness
for myself. I am not concerned with anything. I am not concerned with
making the world a better place. I am not concerned with raising the
poverty level. I am only concerned with my happiness for the rest of the
remaining life which may not be much – though it turned out to be a
lot...

Therefore, I have pursued happiness and I have got the happiness and
what is more, the bonus was that the happiness that I got turned out to
be precisely the enlightenment that I was supposed to seek.

On the basis of the search as I told you, the most important conclusion

I came to is: I am a reasonably comfortable person and I know what pleasure is; even if I were able to enjoy all the pleasures in all the world, with all the intensity, I would still be seeking. So, what is this happiness I am seeking? And the most important conclusion I came to in my personal search for happiness, not enlightenment, is the happiness I am seeking has nothing to do with pleasures in life because I know what pleasure is! Therefore, the happiness I am seeking has nothing to do with the flow of life; flow of life can only mean pleasure or pain.

Therefore, the happiness I am seeking depends entirely on my attitude to life and my attitude to life really means…and that took a long time and lot of misery because attitude to life is too general a concept. What do I mean when I say my 'attitude to life'? And I came to the conclusion that attitude to life means attitude towards the other. From morning till night, what is daily living? Inter-human relationship. The other may be my parent or wife or son or a close relative or a neighbour or someone connected with my business/occupation or someone totally a stranger. Who the other is going to be, at what moment in one's daily living, has never been in anyone's control. Therefore, my question was – what has been my attitude towards the other so far which has not brought me the happiness but unhappiness! And the answer to that, an honest answer to that, was very clear. My attitude towards the other has always been one of fear and rivalry. Fear that he may hurt me, fear that he may take something away from me, fear that he may prevent me from getting what I want because he is also concerned with the same thing and that is why I am not happy.

Therefore, the conclusion I came to is, the happiness I am seeking depends entirely on a harmonious attitude towards the other. I have not been happy so far because my attitude to the other was not harmonious; it was based on fear and rivalry. So, the only way I could have harmonious relationship with the other is if I am able to accept totally that I don't have to fear him.

TIYAMARA So, what led you to that acceptance?

RAMESH   God's Will, my destiny, a happening…So, I came to the conclusion, the other is incapable of harming me. He is incapable of harming me and I am incapable of harming anyone. Therefore, there is no question of carrying any load of hatred for me for my actions or a load of hatred for others, and the disappearance of that suffering, I say, is precisely what enlightenment or my happiness is.

TIYAMARA   You were saying, you reached the point where you realized that no one can hurt you and you can't hurt anyone. So, when people experience hurt, it's simply a lack of acceptance of whatever is!

RAMESH   So, basically, now, we come down to being hurt, mentally or physically. Previously if I was hurt, Tiyamara, what was my reaction? Very simple: he hurt me, I hate him. Now, if I am hurt, what is my reaction? Equally simple but totally different. What has hurt me is a happening which has hurt me because it's my destiny to be hurt according to the Cosmic Law. If it were not my destiny to be hurt according to the Cosmic Law, no power on earth can hurt me. Today if I am hurt, I can understand a happening has hurt me. A happening which hurt me has happened through A, whether it happened through B, C, D, X, Y, Z, my hurt would still be the same. Therefore the change in attitude has been – who has hurt me has now become irrelevant, redundant. The question of who has hurt me simply does not arise. A happening has hurt me because according to a Cosmic Law and my destiny, that happening was supposed to hurt me.

So, you have any more questions? No? Then I will give you one.

TIYAMARA   Okay.

RAMESH   The question is based on the principle, Tiyamara, that even a damn fool will accept a concept which frees him from hatred; hatred for himself and hatred for other, even a damn fool would accept it but the catch is that the concept cannot work until the acceptance is total and not merely intellectual. Therefore, what is Tiyamara's question?

TIYAMARA The question is what can an individual do...to make it the total acceptance and not just the intellectual acceptance?

RAMESH Quite right! In other words, your question is, "What can I do to have the total acceptance that I am not the doer?" Right? I repeat, "What can I do to make my acceptance total that I am not the doer?" Tiyamara, if Tiyamara is not the doer, what the hell can she do? Nothing! You see what I mean? That is the core of the thing, that is the crux of the matter.

TIYAMARA It's got to be something!

RAMESH And that 'something' is not something you can do, but something which can only happen if it is supposed to happen according to Tiyamara's destiny, God's Will / Cosmic Law. That's the crux of the matter. Therefore I said, the one thing that blocks the enlightenment from happening is the conviction that I am in charge of my life.

TIYAMARA What about, you know, I don't know the exact words but the others have said, like Buddha at least says, "You become whatever you meditate upon", "Whatever you bring your attention to, is what you become", which is a little like...I don't know...what do you...

RAMESH I am sorry, I didn't quite get that?

TIYAMARA Well, I have read from the Buddha and he says, "Whatever you attend to or whatever you meditate upon, you become."

RAMESH "Whatever you totally believe, you become." That's what Buddha clearly says. "Whatever you totally believe" – and that's the whole point! How can Tiyamara have the total acceptance that she is not the doer of her deed? It can only happen if it is supposed to happen according to your destiny, God's Will / Cosmic Law.

TIYAMARA Is there anything I can do to...

RAMESH Again, a valid question, Tiyamara! While I am waiting for something to happen, while I am waiting for God to make up his mind, is there not something I can do, with the total acceptance that that is not going to help one way or the other but to pass time, something I can do as a spiritual practice to console my conscience? Valid question! And for that, I do have a suggestion – 'personal investigation'. Personal investigation of a specific action which you are sure is your action.

If you have the time during the day, you can do it at any time. But if you don't have any time during the day, then at the end of the day, take ten minutes off, sit quietly, but again, believing you are not the doer, no reason to be uncomfortable like sitting in a yogic pose with a back straight or anything like that. For my purpose, because it is your personal investigation that you are doing, take the most comfortable seat. And in order to be comfortable, if you would like to have a cup of coffee or a glass of beer or sherry, have it! This is not a discipline! And then do some very simple, what I call 'personal investigation'.

Now, if you go through the various events of the day it will be quite clear, most of the events just happened. You had no control over them. So, from those events, choose only one event, one action, which Tiyamara is sure is her action. In other words, Tiyamara says, "Other actions, I honestly don't know, but this one is my action and I challenge anybody to prove to me that it is not my action." And then investigate that action. Again, very, very simple – if I consider this action as my action, did I decide to do that action at a particular time? If I consider this action as my action, did I decide to do that action at a particular time and then you may remember that, "No, I didn't!"

Then the investigation is, how did the action happen? And you remember, you had a thought and that thought led to your action. If that thought had not happened, your action would not have happened. And you had no control over the happening of that thought. Why? Because no human being ever had any control over what the next thought is going to be! So, if I had no control over the thought and that thought led to the action, how can I call it my action?

So, now, you have done the investigation yourself and have come to the conclusion that the one action that you were so sure is your action turns out, on your own investigation, not to be your action! Then, your acceptance must go considerably deeper. Your intellectual understanding must go much deeper.

Then you take another action and another, and I assure you, however many actions you investigate, every single time, without exception, hundred per cent result, you will keep on coming to the conclusion – not my action, not my action. If I had not happened to be at a certain place, at a certain time and seen something, my action would not have happened. And I had no control over being at that place at that time and much more importantly, for something to happen there and which I happened to see or hear or smell or taste or touch!

And every time, after your own investigation you will come to the conclusion – not my action, not my action. And each time your understanding goes deeper and deeper. Then, at a certain moment of time, depending on your destiny, God's Will / Cosmic Law, a divine flash of total acceptance is likely to happen – "I simply cannot be the doer!" And once that divine flash happens, there will be no more doubts.

TIYAMARA So, for you and your own process, you said that you got disillusioned by your search for enlightenment. Did you then practice this enquiry that you talked about?

RAMESH No, I didn't, personally. You see, the whole point is, for this divine flash of acceptance to happen, you do not necessarily have to go through the process of investigation.

TIYAMARA Right. So, what was your process?

RAMESH It just happened. It just happened on a particular occasion. That particular occasion was, Tiyamara – normally, there were occasions when I used to translate [Nisargadatta] Maharaj's talk and since I had quite a lot to do during my carreer with foreigners and I had a certain command over the English language, the people who came there appreciated my translation. Maharaj knew about it, so he would often ask me to do the translation and in this translation, there was a process, a process in time.

First, I had to listen carefully to what Maharaj said, then understand the significance of it, then translate it into English and then vocalize it into words. So, that was a process. It may have taken only a few seconds, I mean very little time, but still it was a process. But on a particular occasion, I suddenly realized, I could hardly wait for the old man to stop, I knew exactly what he was going to say.

The moment he stopped, the translation poured out. There was clearly no process of translation. And at the end of that morning, someone said, "Ramesh, you were in form today." So, I said, "What do you mean?" He said, "Today, when you were translating, you could hardly wait for Maharaj to stop what he said, and then when you were talking, you were making gestures which you were not making before! It was as if you were not translating but you were the one who was doing the speaking and not Maharaj. You were in form." But I knew what had happened, that there was no translation, everything was happening. And what is more, Maharaj himself noticed that something had happened and he acknowledged it to me.

TIYAMARA So, what did you do? It seems that you spent time in the company of your guru. You spent time in the company of someone with the self-realization and you also…

Ramesh The point I am making is, I already had the conviction that I am not the doer but this just happened to be a proof of what happens, which I didn't need. That is what I am telling you – a proof which I didn't need but it happened. And that's the flash I am referring to!

Okay, Tiyamara?

Tiyamara Yes, thank you!